EMPIRES BESIEGED

TimeFrame AD 200-600

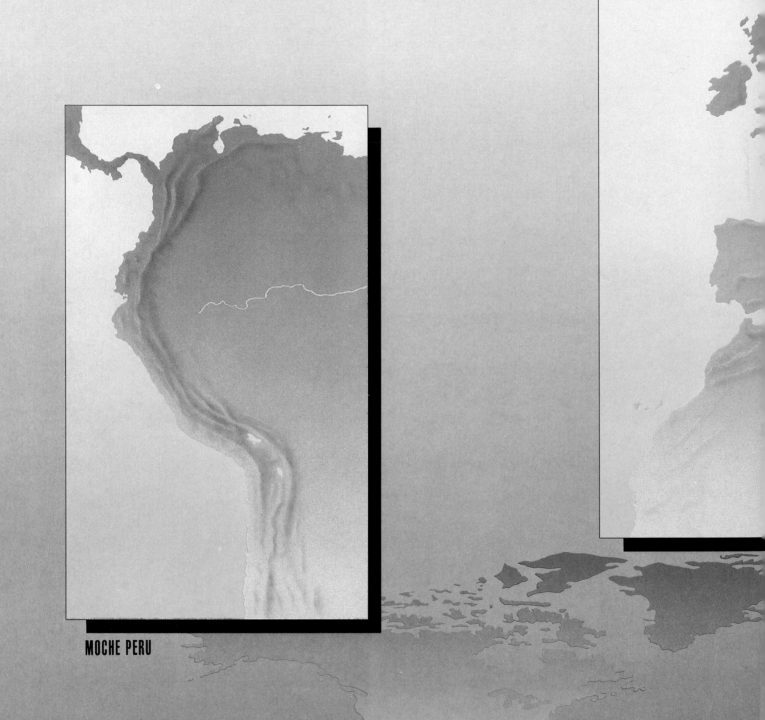

MOCHE PERU

TimeFrame: AD 200-600

THE LATE ROMAN EMPIRE AND SASSANIAN PERSIA

CHINA AND SOUTHEAST ASIA

TIME®
LIFE
BOOKS

Other Publications:
MYSTERIES OF THE UNKNOWN
FIX IT YOURSELF
FITNESS, HEALTH & NUTRITION
SUCCESSFUL PARENTING
HEALTHY HOME COOKING
UNDERSTANDING COMPUTERS
LIBRARY OF NATIONS
THE ENCHANTED WORLD
THE KODAK LIBRARY OF CREATIVE PHOTOGRAPHY
GREAT MEALS IN MINUTES
THE CIVIL WAR
PLANET EARTH
COLLECTOR'S LIBRARY OF THE CIVIL WAR
THE EPIC OF FLIGHT
THE GOOD COOK
WORLD WAR II
HOME REPAIR AND IMPROVEMENT
THE OLD WEST

For information on and a full description of
any of the Time-Life Books series listed above,
please write:
Reader Information
Time-Life Customer Service
P.O. Box C-32068
Richmond, Virginia 23261-2068
or call: 1-800-621-7026

This volume is one in a series that tells the story
of humankind. Other books in the series include:
The Age of God-Kings
Barbarian Tides
A Soaring Spirit
Empires Ascendant

EMPIRES BESIEGED

TimeFrame AD 200-600

BY THE EDITORS OF TIME-LIFE BOOKS

TIME-LIFE BOOKS, ALEXANDRIA, VIRGINIA

Time-Life Books Inc.
is a wholly owned subsidiary of
TIME INCORPORATED

FOUNDER: Henry R. Luce 1898-1967

Editor-in-Chief: Jason McManus
Chairman and Chief Executive Officer:
J. Richard Monroe
President and Chief Operating Officer:
N. J. Nicholas, Jr.
Editorial Director: Ray Cave
Executive Vice President, Books:
Kelso F. Sutton
Vice President, Books: George Artandi

TIME-LIFE BOOKS INC.

EDITOR: George Constable
Executive Editor: Ellen Phillips
Director of Design: Louis Klein
Director of Editorial Resources:
Phyllis K. Wise
Editorial Board: Russell B. Adams, Jr.,
Dale M. Brown, Roberta Conlan,
Thomas H. Flaherty, Lee Hassig, Donia
Ann Steele, Rosalind Stubenberg, Kit van
Tulleken, Henry Woodhead
Director of Photography and Research:
John Conrad Weiser

PRESIDENT: Christopher T. Linen
Chief Operating Officer: John M. Fahey, Jr.
Senior Vice President: James L. Mercer
Vice Presidents: Stephen L. Bair, Ralph J.
Cuomo, Neal Goff, Stephen L. Goldstein,
Juanita T. James, Hallett Johnson III, Car-
ol Kaplan, Susan J. Maruyama, Robert H.
Smith, Paul R. Stewart, Joseph J. Ward
Director of Production Services:
Robert J. Passantino

Editorial Operations
Copy Chief: Diane Ullius
Production: Celia Beattie
Quality Control: James J. Cox (director)
Library: Louise D. Forstall

Correspondents: Elisabeth Kraemer-Singh
(Bonn); Maria Vincenza Aloisi (Paris);
Ann Natanson (Rome). Valuable assis-
tance was also provided by: Mirka Gon-
dicas (Athens); Mona Mortagy (Cairo);
Ara Güler, Suna Güler (Istanbul); Mike
Reid (Lima); Caroline Alcock, Caroline
Lucas, Linda Proud (London); Andrea
Dabrowski (Mexico City); Arti Ahluwa-
lia, Ross Munro (New Delhi); Christina
Lieberman (New York); John Maier, Jr.
(Rio de Janeiro); Ann Wise (Rome); Mary
Johnson (Stockholm); Traudl Lessing
(Vienna).

TIME FRAME

SERIES DIRECTOR: Henry Woodhead
Series Administrator:
Philip Brandt George

Editorial Staff for *Empires Besieged:*
Designer: Dale Pollekoff
Associate Editors: Jim Hicks (text); Robin
Richman (pictures)
Writers: Stephen G. Hyslop, Brian
Pohanka
Researchers: Patricia McKinney (text);
Oobie Gleysteen, Trudy Pearson, Connie
Strawbridge (pictures)
Assistant Designer: Alan Pitts
Copy Coordinator: Jarelle S. Stein
Picture Coordinator: Renée DeSandies
Editorial Assistant: Lona Tavernise

Special Contributors: Ronald H. Bailey,
Champ Clark, George G. Daniels, Brian
McGinn, Charles Phillips, David S.
Thomson, Bryce Walker (text); Marie F.
Taylor Davis, Roxie France-Nuriddin,
Ann-Louise G. Gates, Sandra Maddox,
Jayne Rohrich (research)

CONSULTANTS

The Americas:
DORIE REENTS-BUDET, Professor of Art
History, University of California at Santa
Barbara, Santa Barbara, California

GORDON F. McEWAN, Assistant Cura-
tor, Pre-Columbian Studies, Dumbarton
Oaks, Washington, D.C.

Asia:
JACK L. DULL, Associate Professor of His-
tory, University of Washington, Seattle,
Washington

CHARLES A. PETERSON, Professor of History, Cornell University, Ithaca, New York

India:
VIMALA BEGLEY, Research Associate,
University of Pennsylvania Museum, Iowa
City, Iowa

Persia:
DAVID F. GRAF, Assistant Professor of
History, University of Miami, Coral Ga-
bles, Florida

Roman Empire:
HEINZ CÜPPERS, Director, Rheinishes
Landesmuseum, Trier, Federal Republic of
Germany

WALTER GOFFART, Professor of History,
University of Toronto. Toronto, Canada

**Library of Congress Cataloging in
Publication Data**

Empires besieged
    Bibliography: p.
    Includes index.
    1. History, Ancient. I. Time-Life Books.
D62.E47 1988   930   87-18104
ISBN 0-8094-6416-0
ISBN 0-8094-6417-9 (lib. bdg.)

Time-Life Books Inc. offers a wide range of fine
recordings, including a *Rock 'n' Roll Era* series.
For subscription information, call 1-800-621-
7026 or write Time-Life Music, P.O. Box C-
32068, Richmond, Virginia 23261-2068.

CONTENTS

THE ROMAN DECLINE

Not in centuries, not since the days of Julius Caesar and empire ascendant, had Rome seen such a triumphal homecoming. For too long, the power of Imperial Rome had been on the wane, particularly and assuredly in the west. Barbarian assaults against its far-flung frontiers and revolts among its satellites had combined with disorder and atrophy at home to erode the greatest empire the western world had ever known.

But now, in the year 274 *anno Domini,* the deterioration had been swiftly reversed. In the eyes of the Romans, a young, vigorous, supremely ambitious emperor had restored the western empire to its former majesty. He was Lucius Domitius Aurelianus, known and revered as Aurelian. A man of humble birth from the northeastern province of Dacia Ripensis, he had embarked on a soldier's career, had risen to high rank, and had ultimately won exalted power in the current Roman fashion: through the murder of a predecessor and the elimination of subsequent rivals.

Known to his troops as *Manu ad Ferrum*—Hand on Hilt—Aurelian had first warred with the barbarians along the Danube, driving them back from the frontier; next he had destroyed a barbarian incursion into Italy and then quickly turned his fierce attention to the east. Marching through Syria, he had defeated the forces of a rebellious queen and reduced her Palmyran capital to rubble. Finally, he had gathered his legionaries and marched northwest into Gaul to deal violently with an aggravating Gallic state that had declared its independence from Rome about fifteen years before.

He met the Gauls near Chalons-sur-Marne in 273 and crushed them utterly. Thus, in the space of scarcely five years, Aurelian had welded the fractured empire back together again. No man in living Roman memory had accomplished so much in so short a time. A grateful Senate accorded him the proud title of *Restitutor Orbis*—Restorer of the World.

And now in 274, entering Rome to accept his laurels, Aurelian staged the greatest show the city had witnessed in many decades. The celebration continued for several days, with chariot races in the Circus Maximus and theatrical productions to entertain the citizenry. There were martial games: combat to the death between gladiators, wild animal hunts in a forest specially installed in the arena, even a naval battle among war galleys maneuvering around the flooded Colosseum.

The triumphal parade itself consumed most of the first day and was an event for Romans to cherish. There were three dazzling chariots, symbols of imperial majesty, rolling behind splendid teams of prancing steeds. One chariot was a gift of peace and friendship from the Persian king. The other two were spoils of war from conquered Palmyra, heavy with a great weight of gold and silver and glittering with incrustations of precious stones. The emperor himself, as befitted a conqueror, mounted a war chariot belonging to a Gothic king he had defeated three years before along the Danube. It was drawn by four magnificent stags instead of horses, and in it, Aurelian

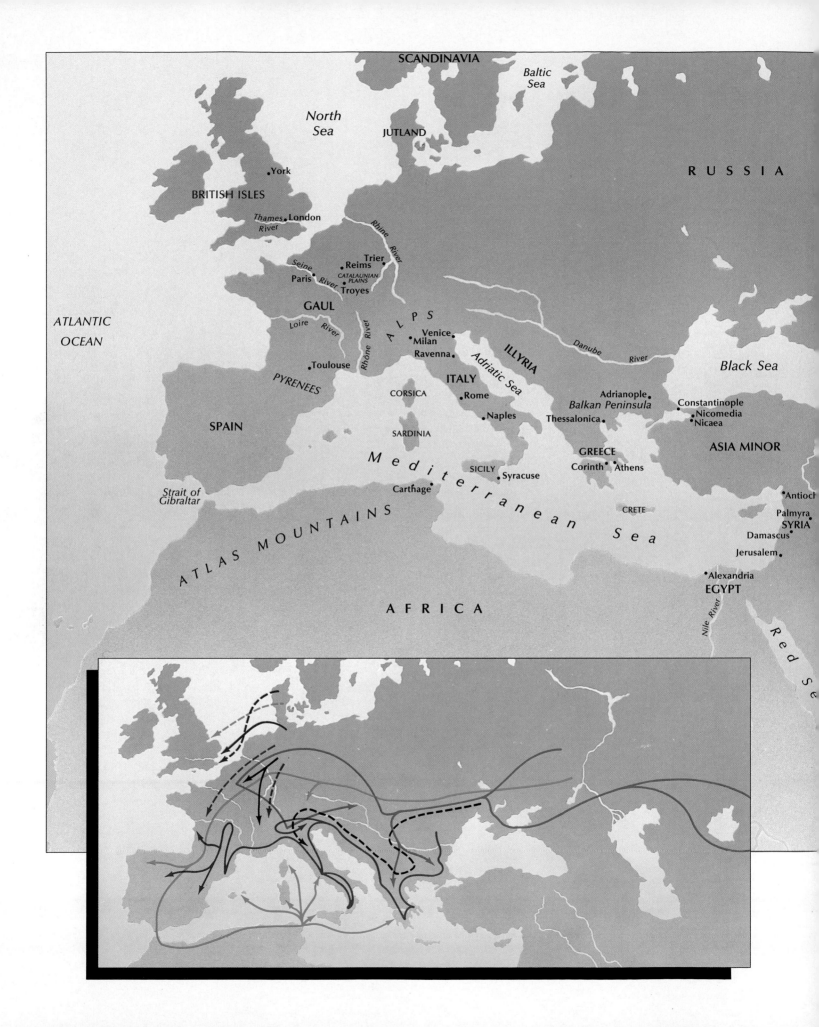

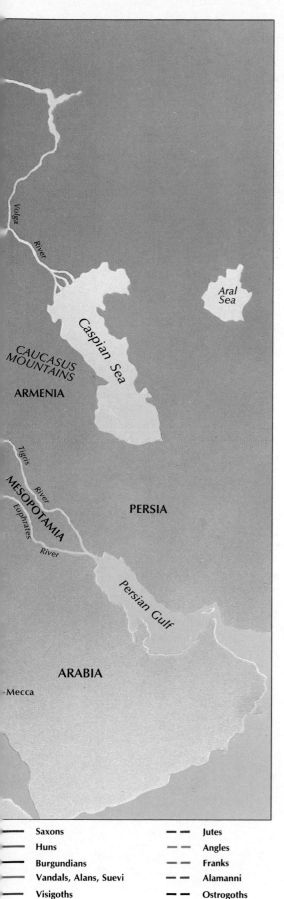

rode past the wildly cheering throngs and up the Capitoline Hill to the temple of Jupiter, center of Roman state religion.

Behind him followed a train of dazzling diversity. No fewer than 1,600 gladiators—soon to display their deadly skills—marched in pairs. There followed a vast menagerie of tigers, elks, giraffes, and elephants, denizens of the subjugated lands. From beyond Rome's borders came representatives of strange and faraway nations, attired in their native garb and bearing treasured gifts to acknowledge the glory of Rome—Arabs from the southern deserts, Blemmyes from Nubia, Axumites from Ethiopia, Hiberians from south of the Caucasus, Saracens, Persians, and Indians. A marcher with a placard identified each nationality.

Rome's prisoners, also identified for the shrieking crowds, were paraded past: German and Asiatic barbarians dressed in animal skins, with their hands tied behind their backs; Goths; Franks; Vandals; the Sarmatians and Roxolani, whose home had been on the Russian steppes; the Juthungi and Alamanni whom Aurelian had crushed when they entered northern Italy and threatened Rome. Along with them shuffled Egyptian rebels, as well as eminent Palmyrans who had been taken captive when Aurelian razed their city.

Among the hapless Palmyrans was their queen, Zenobia, whom Aurelian had captured while destroying her upstart empire. To the vulgar jeers of the crowd, she staggered along, bowed under the heavy golden chains encircling her arms, legs, and neck and encumbered by a costume bearing such an immense weight of jewels that she could scarcely move. Wrote the historian Pollio, with some sympathy: "She was adorned with gems so huge that she labored under the weight of her ornaments, for it is said that this woman, courageous though she was, halted very frequently, saying that she could not endure the load of her gems."

Such was the triumph of Aurelian. Yet all his seeming invincibility and all Rome's newfound good fortune were but an illusion, the briefest and most temporary of respites, a mere twitch in the inexorable course of history. Within a year, Aurelian was dead, slain by some disaffected soldiers while preparing a campaign against Persia. And Rome, which had not—perhaps could not—purge the poisons of its lengthy and growing illness, was again slipping into a decline, beset by barbarians and riven by political, religious, military, and social upheavals. From time to time, under the prod of exceptional leaders like Aurelian, Rome would briefly rouse itself like some great beast, only to fall back weaker than before.

Rome was not alone in its plight. In the years between AD 200 and 600, empires were under siege all across the broad civilized belt that stretched from Rome in the west to China in the east. The classical world was enveloped by chaos and on the verge of collapse.

After nearly 400 years of enlightened rule, China's Han dynasty was shattered by court intrigues that led, early in the third century AD, to vicious civil wars. Amid all the resultant confusion, Hunnish, Mongol, and Turkish nomads flooded out of the Asian steppes and, in a bewildering variety of shifting coalitions, established a splintered mastery over Manchuria and over northern China.

In the turmoil of the time, Confucianism, the state doctrine of the Hans, faded

By the end of the sixth century AD, the Roman Empire in the west had been ravaged repeatedly by barbarian invasions (map inset). The empire's traditional river boundaries—the Rhine and Danube—had failed to contain the onslaught, and the city of Rome had been sacked. But the Roman Empire in the east—that domain destined to bear the name Byzantium, with its capital at Constantinople—controlled a vast expanse, which included Asia Minor, Syria, western Arabia, Egypt, and coastal North Africa.

—— Saxons   – – Jutes

—— Huns   – – Angles

—— Burgundians   – – Franks

—— Vandals, Alans, Suevi   – – Alamanni

—— Visigoths   – – Ostrogoths

before the promises of salvation that were offered by Buddhism, transported into China by Indian monks and merchants. Yet through it all, Chinese culture not only survived but expanded: The barbarian overlords of the north were gradually assimilated by the Chinese, refugees from the barbarian rule carried the learning of the Hans into the backward south, and Buddhist missionaries introduced Chinese civilization to the Korean peninsula and the island of Japan.

In the interior of Eurasia's civilized swath, India's destiny was closely linked to the resurgent military prowess of neighboring Persia. In the middle of the third century AD, northern India's Kushan rulers were toppled by Persia's newly installed and highly aggressive Sassanian regime. Out of the prolonged disorder that followed, there finally emerged the great Gupta dynasty, which by the fifth century would bring all of northern India, from the Himalayas to the Narmada River and from the Bay of Bengal to the Arabian Sea, under its sway.

Sheltered by the Himalayas and buffered from barbarian invasion by Persian frontier forces to the northwest, the Guptas presided over a halcyon era of Indian culture: Hinduism, with its aristocratic accents, overshadowed Buddhism; Sanskrit, neglected for 700 years, exploded in an extraordinary literary revival; science flourished and Indian traders planted satellite states in Southeast Asia and Indonesia. Then, toward the close of the fifth century, while the Persians were preoccupied by their ceaseless conflict with the Roman Empire, Hunnish barbarians broke through the Iranian shield, invaded northwest India, and after years of fighting, toppled the Guptas.

To the east, an emerging Persian dynasty sought to recapture the past. Founded by a rural lord who came to power by the simple expedient of clubbing his Parthian overlord to death, the Sassanian dynasty consolidated and expanded its empire by appealing to Persian traditions that invoked the glories of Cyrus and Darius. Steeped in the ritual splendor of oriental despots, Persia's Sassanian rulers revived the moribund creed of Zoroastrianism, making it the official state religion and part of the regime's administrative and judicial apparatus.

Yet their implacable hostility toward Rome—the two empires fought more than a dozen wars—eventually sapped the strength of the Sassanids, and they were overrun by the so-called White Huns. A terrible century of vassalage followed.

And then there was the decline and fall of Rome itself.

In the gray dawn of the calamitous third century, the perimeters of the Roman Empire extended 10,000 miles, beginning in the west with the defensive wall raised across Britain by the emperor Hadrian. On the continental landmass, the frontiers of Rome twisted south from the North Sea, along the Rhine River, then reached east along the Danube to the Black Sea and thence, behind the barrier of the Caucasus Mountains, to the Caspian Sea. Hooking to the southeast through the Middle East, the line encompassed Asia Minor and Egypt before thrusting west along the North African coast to the shores of the Atlantic.

Pressing hard against the far banks of the Rhine and the Danube, often within view of the legionaries who manned the garrisons, were the rude settlements of the barbarians, peoples from southern Scandinavia and Jutland who had slowly and haltingly trekked by various routes to the frontiers of the Roman Empire. The northerners were no strangers to Rome: Marius, that grim old soldier of the republic, had warred against them as early as 102 BC, and Julius Caesar had briefly ventured beyond the Rhine to fight them in their forests and swamps.

The earliest barbarian forces that waged war against Rome fought in ragged ranks and units, displaying a lack of discipline that cost them dearly in contests with the well-drilled Roman legions. Even so, they were not without soldierly assets; their zest for the fight, combined with their superb horsemanship and skill at hit-and-run tactics, made them worthy foes. Among the barbarians every able-bodied man was a soldier, loyal to his tribe or clan, and bonded by oath to serve a tribal leader, such as the chieftain shown here—an Ostrogoth armed with a spear and a long slashing sword known as a spatha.

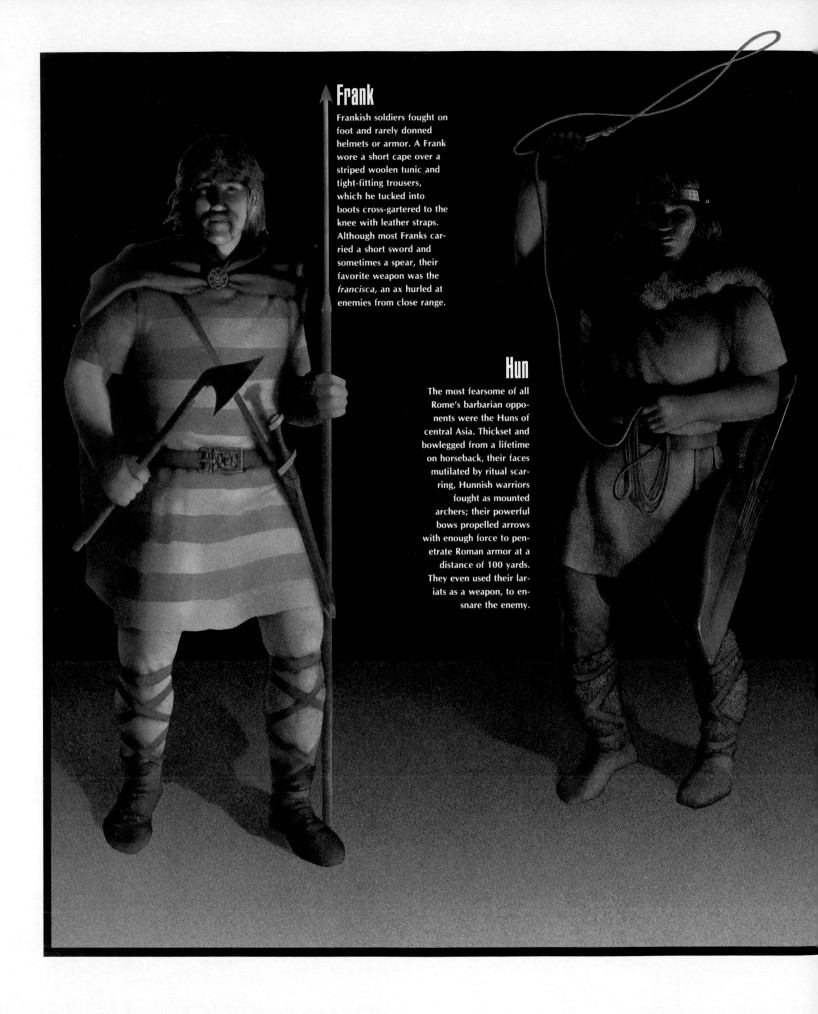

Frank

Frankish soldiers fought on foot and rarely donned helmets or armor. A Frank wore a short cape over a striped woolen tunic and tight-fitting trousers, which he tucked into boots cross-gartered to the knee with leather straps. Although most Franks carried a short sword and sometimes a spear, their favorite weapon was the *francisca*, an ax hurled at enemies from close range.

Hun

The most fearsome of all Rome's barbarian opponents were the Huns of central Asia. Thickset and bowlegged from a lifetime on horseback, their faces mutilated by ritual scarring, Hunnish warriors fought as mounted archers; their powerful bows propelled arrows with enough force to penetrate Roman armor at a distance of 100 yards. They even used their lariats as a weapon, to ensnare the enemy.

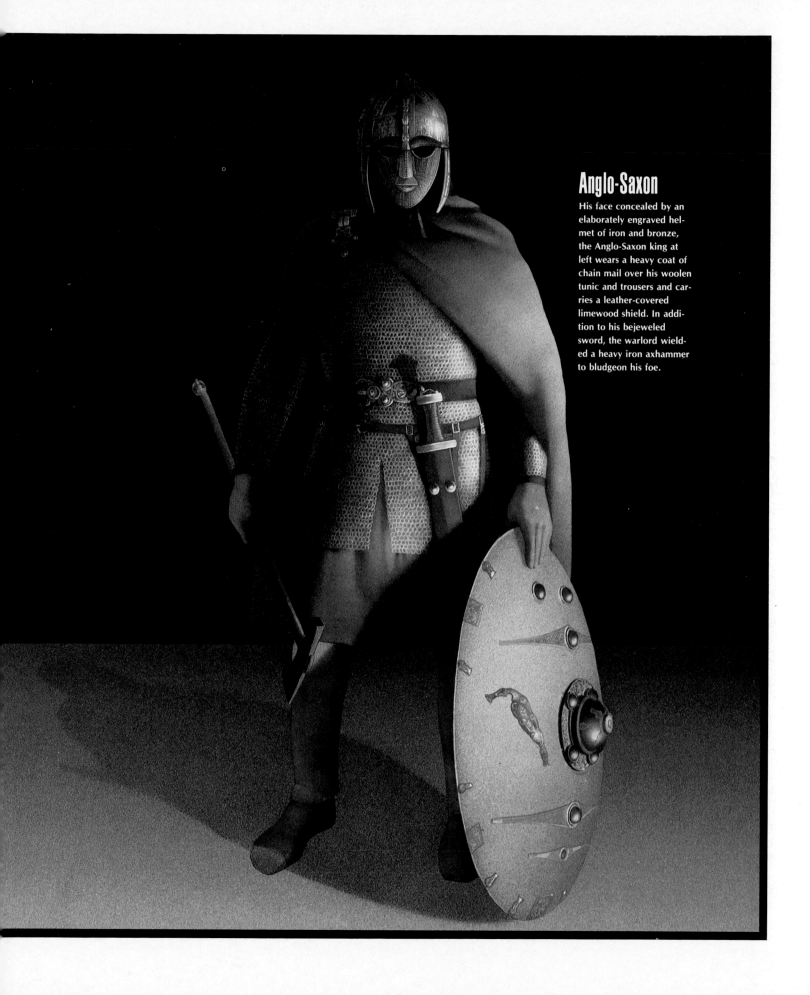

Anglo-Saxon

His face concealed by an elaborately engraved helmet of iron and bronze, the Anglo-Saxon king at left wears a heavy coat of chain mail over his woolen tunic and trousers and carries a leather-covered limewood shield. In addition to his bejeweled sword, the warlord wielded a heavy iron axhammer to bludgeon his foe.

Despite all discouragements, the barbarians grew stronger, and their loose tribal groupings gradually took coherent form until, during the third century, Rome's defenders were confronted, from west to east, by Franks on the lower Rhine, the Alamanni confederation in central Germany, Vandals in Hungary, and most formidable of them all, Goths, who dominated southern Russia. Behind them were other tribes that would one day make names for themselves—Saxons on the Weser River, Burgundians on the Main, Lombards in Silesia.

Farmers and herdsmen by necessity, the tribesmen were warriors by instinct and inclination. The Roman historian Tacitus described them as a robust race with "blue eyes and reddish hair; great bodies, especially powerful for attack" who considered it "limp and slack to get with the sweating of your brow what you can gain with the shedding of your blood."

Their social organization was geared for fighting. The basic unit was the clan, a number of families whose warriors periodically gathered to approve the decisions of an elected leader by thwacking their spears against their shields. Gradually, larger bands were formed through alliances cemented by marriage, the exchange of gifts, or simple expediency. Chiefs and even kings emerged, surrounding themselves with retinues of warriors who had sworn an oath of loyalty in return for a share of loot.

Yet for all their zeal, the Germanic tribesmen were little more than a rabble. Lacking armor, they hurled themselves screaming and half-naked into battle behind wooden or wicker shields. Only a few possessed swords, at least in the early years; the rest relied on clubs or wooden lances whose points had been hardened by fire.

When such barbarian mobs met the highly disciplined, heavily armed Roman legions, the result was almost always a rout. On one such occasion, wrote a Roman historian, fleeing barbarians who attempted to swim a river to safety "were battered by javelins, or carried away by the current, or finally overwhelmed by the mass of fugitives and collapse of the river banks. Some ignominiously tried to escape by climbing trees. As they cowered among the branches, bowmen amused themselves by shooting them down."

And so, for at least the first half of the third century, the barbarians were held largely at arm's length, restlessly roaming the far banks of the Rhine and the Danube and all the while growing in numbers and hostile intent, a severe burden on a Roman Empire already on the verge of collapse from its own internal disorders.

These were great. The government of Rome had reached the depths of corruption. As he lay dying in AD 211, the emperor Septimius Severus offered a succinct piece of advice to his sons: "Enrich the soldiers, despise all others!" Severus knew exactly what he was talking about: He had himself won the throne of the Roman Empire through the strength of his loyal soldiers after the chaotic and bloody decades that followed the reign of Marcus Aurelius.

Worn by the cares of his office, Marcus Aurelius had died while engaged in a campaign against the tribes on the Danube. He was succeeded by his son Commodus, a vile young man who somehow survived on the throne for a dozen years, meanwhile murdering his sister and various critics and, it was said, setting up voluptuous housekeeping with 300 prostitutes and an equal number of boys. The frightful reign came to an end only after the emperor's own praetorian prefect arranged to have him strangled by a professional wrestler named Narcissus.

There followed a tragicomic interlude: Pertinax, a distinguished old general, was named emperor by the Praetorian Guard despite his protest that the honor was "not an attractive proposition." After he was installed, Pertinax made the mistake of trying to reestablish control over the praetorians, even cutting back on their emoluments; as might be expected, a number of infuriated guardsmen invaded the palace and hacked the old man to death.

Once that deed was done, the praetorians decided to auction off the imperial succession. According to a third-century account, a wealthy senator named Didius Julianus was "holding a drinking bout" when his wife, daughters, and fellow celebrants persuaded him to hurry to the barracks where the sale was taking place. Consequently, after spirited bidding, supreme power in the Roman Empire fell to Didius Julianus for the immense sum of 25,000 sesterces per praetorian—an amount equal to six times his annual salary.

On the empire's frontiers, fighting soldiers were understandably outraged at the news of the bargaining. The commander of the Danube legions was Lucius Septimius Severus, who marched with his army to Rome. The terrified emperor, abandoned by everyone, bolted his palace doors and retired to his bedchamber, where a soldier, with one swipe of his sword, soon put an end to Julianus's pretentions.

A stern old soldier who had been born in Rome's African province (he would claim that he carried in his veins the blood of Carthaginian nobility), Severus was hailed as emperor by his army; but Rome's legions in Britain and Syria had other ideas, each of them claiming the throne for their own commander. It would take four years of brutal civil war before Septimius Severus finally wrested clear title.

As emperor, Severus suffered no illusions as to the source of his power. He raised the pay of his soldiers by one-third and offered special retirement benefits for loyal service; he also allowed the men to marry and to farm small plots of public land in the vicinity of their camps.

Yet having secured his base of power, Septimus Severus proceeded to use it unwisely. He attacked the eastern empire of the Parthian monarchy, thereby setting in motion a series of events that would prove damaging to Rome. So weakened were the Parthian rulers by the Roman campaigns that within three decades they were overthrown by an ambitious young nobleman from the Iranian highlands whose goal was nothing less than the re-creation of the ancient Persian empire. The noble's name was Ardashir, and in AD 230, only six years after seizing power, he took the first step along his fateful path by invading Roman Syria and Mesopotamia. Thus began a succession of wars that would eventually exhaust the resources of both Imperial Rome and Sassanian Persia.

The Romans mustered three field armies. They were commanded by the young emperor Alexander Severus—no kin to Septimius, who was by now dead. Indeed, Alexander was one of a growing number of outlanders among Rome's ruling class, being of Syrian birth. In his war against Ardashir, Alexander could earn no better than a stalemate. Yet hardly had an uneasy truce fallen upon the Persian front than Alexander Severus was called to the north, where the Germanic Alamanni, taking advantage of Roman preoccupations in the east, had burst across the Rhine. At that moment of crisis, Alexander either wilted or lost confidence in his troops. In any case, he determined to bribe the barbarians rather than fight them; then, incredibly, he apparently forgot Septimus's dictum and attempted to make up for the loss of funds by slashing his army's payroll—a foolish mistake that resulted in his death at the hands of his angry soldiers.

Roman cavalry led by Emperor Marcus Aurelius (at center, wearing a crested helmet) fight bearded barbarians
in this spirited relief from a second-century sarcophagus. Aurelius spent the last fourteen years of his reign in
continual warfare against Germanic tribes on the Danube and was with his army when he died of disease in
AD 180 at the age of fifty-nine.

These Roman coins depict emperors Septimius Severus *(top)* and Diocletian *(bottom),* both strong-willed military men who were elevated to power by the mandate of their legions. Severus, who became emperor in AD 193 and ruled for eighteen years, rewarded his loyal subordinates and ruthlessly eliminated his rivals, among them twenty-nine members of the Roman Senate. The formidable Diocletian, who reigned from 284 to 305, initiated wide-ranging reforms, dividing imperial power among a tetrarchy and creating an eastern capital at Nicomedia in Asia Minor.

With Alexander's death in AD 235, the Roman Empire entered a half century of military anarchy in which more than twenty rulers rose and fell in bewildering succession. Nearly all these so-called barracks emperors were military commanders, often of humble provincial origin, who were elevated to power by their armies and swiftly removed for one reason or another.

In this time of turmoil, the Rhine-Danube frontiers were dangerously neglected, offering opportunities the barbarian tribes were quick to exploit. In 251, Visigoths burst across the Danube and swarmed into the Balkans, where they were met by a Roman force under the emperor Decius, who had only recently scrambled to the throne. He did not live to enjoy it. Blundering into a marsh, he led his legions to slaughter, and he himself earned the dubious distinction of becoming the first Roman emperor to die in battle with the barbarians.

Disaster followed disaster: Alamanni warriors pushed through the gap between the Rhine and the Danube, seized southwestern Germany, and repeatedly raided northern Italy, reaching as far as Milan. Meanwhile, Franks on the Rhine raided Gaul and may even have penetrated into Spain. With Rome's emperors unable to stem the onslaught, the legions of Gaul, Spain, and Britain in AD 259 acclaimed as emperor a general named Postumus, who fought the barbarians to a standstill until he, too, was murdered by his soldiery.

In the east, the Roman Empire had suffered even deeper humiliation. There, the Sassanian king Shapur annexed Armenia, invaded Mesopotamia, and led an army into Syria once again. Although sorely distracted by barbarian assaults on other fronts, the current emperor Valerian had little choice except to defend his bountiful eastern holdings. Once on the scene, however, Valerian's army—weakened by a plague— seemed unequal to the task, and the elderly Valerian apparently sought to buy his way out of the dilemma by offering an immense tribute. In response, Shapur demanded that Valerian himself be present at the negotiations—and, when the emperor appeared, he was treacherously taken prisoner and held for the rest of his life.

Faced with what seemed to be a hopeless situation, Valerian's son, co-emperor, and successor, Gallienus, turned the defense of the eastern provinces over to one Odenathus, a Romanized Arab noble and self-styled King of Palmyra, a city in Syria. Odenathus had rallied local forces against Shapur, and now, astonishingly, he managed to hurl back the Persian advance. He remained loyal to Rome for as long as he lived, but after his death in 267, his widow, Zenobia, acting as regent for her son, seceded from Rome and set up an independent Palmyran empire, which in its brief heyday included a huge portion of Rome's eastern territories. Thus, at the low ebb of his reign, Gallienus could realistically claim to control little more than a small fraction of the old Roman Empire—Italy, Illyria, and the coastal belt of North Africa.

Yet even in that despairing moment, Rome's military fortunes began to turn. Gallienus, a willing fighter, somehow managed for seven years to fend off repeated attacks along the frontiers. And after his death—inevitably at the hand of his officers— the agonizing job of patching the old empire back together was undertaken by a series of hard-bitten, remarkably able emperors, who vanquished the Goths in the Balkans, cleared Gaul of its Frankish and Alamanni invaders, and campaigned successfully against Sassanian Persia. Among these leaders was the illustrious Aurelian, who for a fleeting moment restored the empire in the west to much of its Augustan glory. In truth, however, the structure of the empire had been irreversibly corroded.

Rome's economy, for instance, was a shambles. In most ancient societies, monetary systems were based on the reasonable assumption that the value of coins depended on their precious-metal content. Yet in order to meet the enormous costs of their incessant wars and the demands of their citizens for services, Rome's emperors repeatedly debased their currency until, during the regime of Gallienus, the basic unit, the supposedly silver denarius, was in reality 95 percent copper, with only a thin silver coating.

As the value of money tumbled, prices inexorably rose—to the point that a measure of wheat worth one-half of a denarius in the second century now cost 100 denarii. Among those most hurt by the the inflationary spiral was, of course, the government itself: As the real value of their tax revenues eroded, emperors were ever more compelled to meet the needs of the armies through direct requisition from the civilian population of such vital commodities as food, clothing, and wagons.

Meanwhile, the empire's productive capacities plunged. With the loss, however temporary, of such territories as Gaul, Spain, and the Palmyran east, the natural resources available for production were vastly diminished. Compounding the predicament, the human casualties suffered in constant conflict, the ravenous hunger of the military for replacement drafts, and the recurrent ravages of plague had seriously depleted the empire's working population.

Perhaps worst of all was a flight of peasants from the land: With their crops subject to confiscation and with their property vulnerable to the depredations not only of barbarians but of marauding Roman soldiers, thousands of farmers either sought safety in the walled cities along the frontiers or turned to a more profitable vocation—brigandage. Their abandoned fields returned to wilderness.

The empire had reached a low ebb. Yet from its earliest days, Rome had always found a leader who was prepared to take whatever drastic action was required to rescue it from even the direst of difficulties. Aurelian had been such a man. And again came a powerful leader. On November 17, 284, a Roman army near Nicomedia on the shores of Asia Minor acclaimed as emperor a general named Gaius Aurelius Valerius Diocletianus—who would become renowned as Diocletian.

A complex and often contradictory man, Diocletian was born of common stock as the son of a Dalmatian peasant. But as an emperor, he realized almost instinctively that it was vital to invest his rule with the sort of supreme majesty that would shield it from below. Claiming a divine right to rule as the pagan Jupiter's agent on earth, he insisted on being addressed as Lord instead of First Citizen, the title that had been customary since the time of Augustus. The trend toward absolutism had been evident for years; Diocletian merely made it a matter of law and used it to distance himself still further from would-be assassins.

In emulation of Persia's Sassanian monarchs, he dwelled in oriental splendor, surrounding himself with eunuchs, donning a diadem, adorning himself in raiment of purple and gold silk, and wearing red buskins encrusted with precious stones. Borrowing another Sassanian trait, Diocletian demanded that all people admitted to his presence—including the members of his own family—prostrate themselves and kiss the hem of his robe.

Yet Diocletian understood only too well that the burdens of his beleaguered empire were far too weighty for the shoulders of a single man. In the summer of 285, he therefore promoted another general—Maximian—to the position of caesar, a sort of vice-emperor, and a year later to full imperial equality with the title of Augustus. Under the plan, Diocletian would be responsible for the eastern provinces, with

Emperor Constantine I is shown on a coin *(top)* in symbolic partnership with the Greek king Alexander. Like Alexander, Constantine's achievements earned him the sobriquet "the Great"; similarly, both men's heirs failed to meet their predecessors' expectations. After his father's death in AD 337, Constans I *(bottom)* warred with his two elder brothers for control of the empire. He was assassinated during a military revolt in 350.

residence in Nicomedia, while Maximian would take charge of matters in the west.

The historic city of Rome had long been fading in importance and henceforth would languish as an administrative backwater in the affairs of the Roman Empire. Both Diocletian and Maximian established mobile imperial courts, or comitatuses, and moved with them wherever and whenever necessity dictated. For instance, in order that he might be closer to the areas threatened by barbarian incursion, Maximian established Milan as his Italian headquarters and Trier as his base in Gaul.

Apparently, both Diocletian and Maximian were pleased by the way their partnership was working. At any rate, a few years later Diocletian went even further by elevating two younger men to the rank of caesar. One of them, Galerius, would act as assistant to Diocletian, with specific responsibility for most of the Balkans. The other caesar, Constantius, was Maximian's heir designate, with authority over Gaul and Britain. To cement the relationship, each of the emperors adopted his associate as son. Each of the younger men, in turn, was required to marry a daughter of his patron. Diocletian remained dominant in the so-called tetrarchy and held major responsibility for both the successes and the failures of the regime.

Among the early orders of business for the leaders was military reform and reorganization. The size of the army was doubled, and conscription was initiated. It was obvious that static defense of the empire's long frontier was inadequate against the

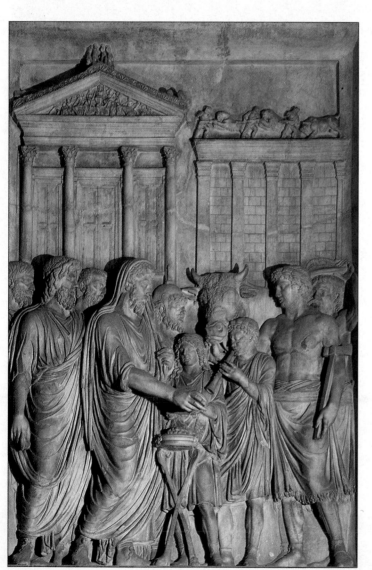

Emperor Marcus Aurelius, the hooded figure at center, offers incense at the beginning of a religious rite at the Temple of Jupiter in Rome, while senators and temple officials look on next to a sacrificial bull. Marcus Aurelius, a follower of Stoicism, eloquently expressed the precepts of that austere philosophy in his famous *Meditations.* He was also a stern supporter of traditional pagan religious beliefs and instigated persecutions of the empire's Christian minority.

movements of the barbarians. Adopting a promising earlier idea, Diocletian and his colleagues created mobile field armies under the command of *magistri militum,* or "masters of soldiery," and they held these forces in reserve, ready to counterattack whenever and wherever the barbarians threatened major breakthroughs. Moreover, following the Persian example, the Roman armies increasingly relied on formations of well-armed and extremely mobile cavalry.

Diocletian and his lieutenants recorded victory after victory with a military force whose total numbers had soared to almost 500,000 men. Maximian defeated Alammani and Frankish warriors in Gaul, and he suppressed a rebellion in Mauretania; Constantius voyaged to Britain, where he quashed the pretensions of a usurper, then returned to Gaul and drove back invading Alamanni tribesmen; Galerius campaigned profitably on the Danube, and in 298, he dramatically defeated Persia's King Narses.

The cost of the army and its achievements was astronomical, and Diocletian took on the seemingly impossible job of finding ways to finance it all in an empire already verging on bankruptcy. In addition to ruthless direct requisition, he reformed the monetary system by minting coins with a respectable measure of gold and silver. Next, he expanded the tax structure by collecting taxes on tracts of land according to their size, fertility, and produce. In addition, agricultural landholders were required to pay a head tax on all animals and workers. (Women counted for only a half-head each.) Since 90 percent of the empire was rural, taxes were generally paid in units of grain or other commodities; landless wage earners and shopkeepers paid what they were assessed in currency. In the empire's towns, well-to-do councillors, known as curials, were made responsible for tax collection—and obliged to pay any deficits in the community quota out of their own pockets.

Yet despite the heavy taxes, inflation continued to eat at the economy. Blaming the deadly spiral on the "furious avarice" of merchants, Diocletian in 302 froze both wages and prices—with death the penalty for violations. The items earmarked for price ceilings, listed on stone tablets throughout the empire, offer a glimpse of the variety of Roman life—including the fattened turtledoves and goldfinches that were consumed as delicacies by the elite, figs from Syria and wine from Egypt, underclothes fashioned from hare's fur, and parchment treated with saffron. As it happened, the freeze was ineffective: Goods were withdrawn, a black market prospered, and apparently Diocletian quietly let the matter drop.

To administer its edicts, the regime relied on a huge and pervasive bureaucracy from which the military was increasingly excluded. For greater efficiency and to prevent any provincial governor from gaining too much power, the number of provinces was nearly doubled to create more than 100 smaller units, which were in turn grouped in twelve administrative dioceses. Although provincial governors retained judicial as well as executive authority, their decisions could in fact be appealed by diocesan vicars directly to the emperor.

True power, of course, stemmed from the top, where the emperor was advised by the Sacred Consistory, composed of such officials as the Count of Sacred Gifts, who was in effect the empire's treasurer; the Master of Offices, who presided over the secretariat; and, not least, the Supervisor of the Sacred Bedchamber, a eunuch who managed the imperial living quarters and was widely considered to be an official of great and sinister influence. Even more menacing was an army of functionaries— *agentes in rebus*—who kept an eye on the affairs of citizens in addition to performing their regular duties.

Diocletian's measures were strong medicine, and they provided at least a temporary remedy for the economic and military afflictions that had befallen the empire. To achieve success, he had placed great stress on imperial unity and conformity under the law among all factions and citizens. Thus it was that in the waning years of his reign, the normally tolerant Diocletian came into terrible conflict with the Christian church and its doctrines.

Diocletian's religion was the ancient pagan cult, with its pantheon of divinities and rituals that were inextricably intertwined with the Roman state. The emperor came to regard the Christians, not as an invigorating new force within the empire, but as divisive traitors to Rome.

The blow fell without warning on the morning of February 23, 303, when imperial soldiers in Nicomedia swooped down on a Christian church within clear view of Diocletian's palace, putting it to the torch and feeding its Holy Scriptures to the flames. The first edict, dated that very day, ordered the closing of all churches throughout the empire; their scriptures would be turned over to the state for burning. A second edict commanded Christian clergy to make sacrifices to pagan gods on pain of death—an order that was soon extended to all Christians, including Diocletian's own wife and daughter. Diocletian clearly meant business, and when an outraged Christian in Nicomedia tore down an official proclamation he was, according to a Christian chronicler, "duly roasted, exhibiting marvelous endurance throughout, and finally burnt to ashes."

So began a savage persecution against the practitioners of a religion that had made notable advances in the Roman Empire. Viewed in its early days as a mutation of Judaism, Christianity had been generally tolerated except for a few instances of persecutions that, while ugly enough, were local in nature and of relatively brief duration. Not until AD 250 and the reign of the emperor Decius did a Roman ruler embark upon an empire-wide anti-Christian campaign, and even then it was possible to escape. One of its most prominent targets, Bishop Cyprian of Carthage, avoided its reach by going into hiding for a while. Once Decius was dead, Cyprian returned to public view and resumed his religious activities. A few years later, however, during a similar campaign of persecution undertaken by the emperor Valerian, the stubborn Cyprian was hunted down and beheaded.

By making Christianity a scapegoat for the myriad misfortunes of their reigns, Decius and Valerian had apparently hoped to propitiate the pagan gods. Yet Decius, slain in battle by barbarians, and Valerian, taken captive by the Persians, had both come to bad ends—a fact that Christians were undoubtedly quick to attribute to the wrath of their own god. Whatever the case, succeeding emperors, preoccupied with far greater problems, had allowed the young religion to spread largely unchecked for nearly a half-century.

As Christianity spread, its doctrines took shape, borrowing not only from Judaism but from many of the precepts of Greek philosophy and assimilating and transforming pagan rituals and observances. For example, although the date of Christ's birth was unknown, Christians celebrated it on December 25, a day coinciding with the winter solstice and with the birthday of the sun god Mithras much favored by Romans. The Christians also gained numerous adherents for their good works, supplying food for the needy, providing burial for the destitute, and on occasion even ransoming captives held by barbarians.

In launching his anti-Christian campaign, Diocletian, aging, ailing, and weary from his long years of travail, may have finally succumbed to the nagging efforts of his junior colleague. Galerius, in particular, was a fervent believer in conformity and a bitter enemy of Christianity. Indeed, it was Galerius who issued the edict imposing the death penalty for failure to worship pagan gods.

At all events, the suppression proceeded with ferocious energy. Throughout the empire, churches were burned and churchmen thrown into dungeons. One of them, a Bishop Donatus, spent six years behind bars and endured the agonies of the rack nine times. (He survived to lead a protest against the readmission to the church of those who had, unlike himself, recanted their faith.) Thousands were executed without trial and with little regard for rank. Diocletian's chamberlain, Peter, was publicly tortured and killed along with such high court officials as Gorgonius and Dorotheus. In Phrygia, when the inhabitants of a small town declared their loyalty to Christianity, they were herded into their church, which was then set afire by soldiers.

Diocletian's official sponsorship of the anti-Christian campaign had been in effect for little more than a year when the Roman world was stunned by the news that he and his senior partner, Maximian, would soon abdicate as Augusti—in favor of their juniors, Constantius and Galerius, who would in turn name two younger associates to serve as caesars. For Christians and Christianity, the accession of the implacable Galerius was if anything a turn for the worse. The oppression continued, and relief came only after six frightful years, when, as he lay dying, Galerius apparently realized that Christianity was too widespread to be stamped out and that his excesses were

The ebb and flow of the various conquering armies imbued the desert cities of ancient Syria with a curiously hybrid culture that was uniquely their own. Crossroads of trade between Rome and the kingdoms of far-off Asia, these outposts of civilization were also fertile intersections of language, art, and religion.

The city of Dura-Europus, which stood on the western bank of the Euphrates River at the edge of the Arabian desert, was typical of these communities on the frontiers of the Roman and Parthian empires. Eu-ropus was established in 300 BC as a Macedonian military base and became a center of Hellenistic culture in the Middle East.

During the fragmentation of Alexander's empire, the Seleucids wrested control of the city and renamed it Dura—the Babylonian word for "fortress." Next a Parthian stronghold, the city survived intermittent warfare between Parthian and Roman armies to become an important layover on the caravan route from the east.

Dura-Europus was home to a multilingual population of Greek, Roman, Parthian, and Semitic origin and was noted for its numerous religious shrines. These included a Jewish synagogue and Christian church as well as temples honoring a multitude of pagan deities, many of them composites of Roman and eastern gods.

The fate of this thriving colony was a tragic one. Sometime prior to AD 260, Dura-Europus, now in Roman hands, was besieged and captured by a massive army of Sassanian Persians. Its citizens were killed or sold into slavery, and the city abandoned to the desert

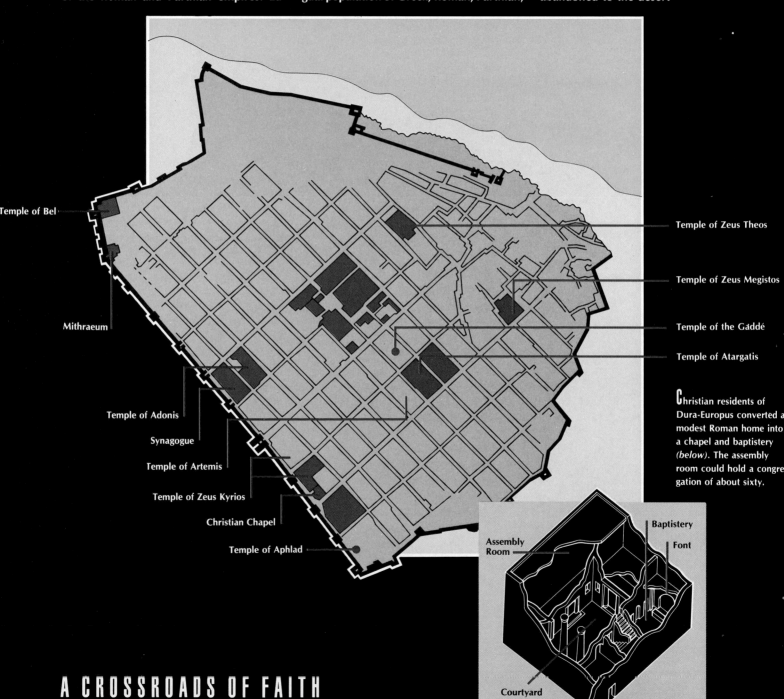

Temple of Bel

Mithraeum

Temple of Adonis

Synagogue

Temple of Artemis

Temple of Zeus Kyrios

Christian Chapel

Temple of Aphlad

Temple of Zeus Theos

Temple of Zeus Megistos

Temple of the Gáddé

Temple of Atargatis

Christian residents of Dura-Europus converted a modest Roman home into a chapel and baptistery (below). The assembly room could hold a congregation of about sixty.

Baptistery

Font

Assembly Room

Courtyard

A CROSSROADS OF FAITH

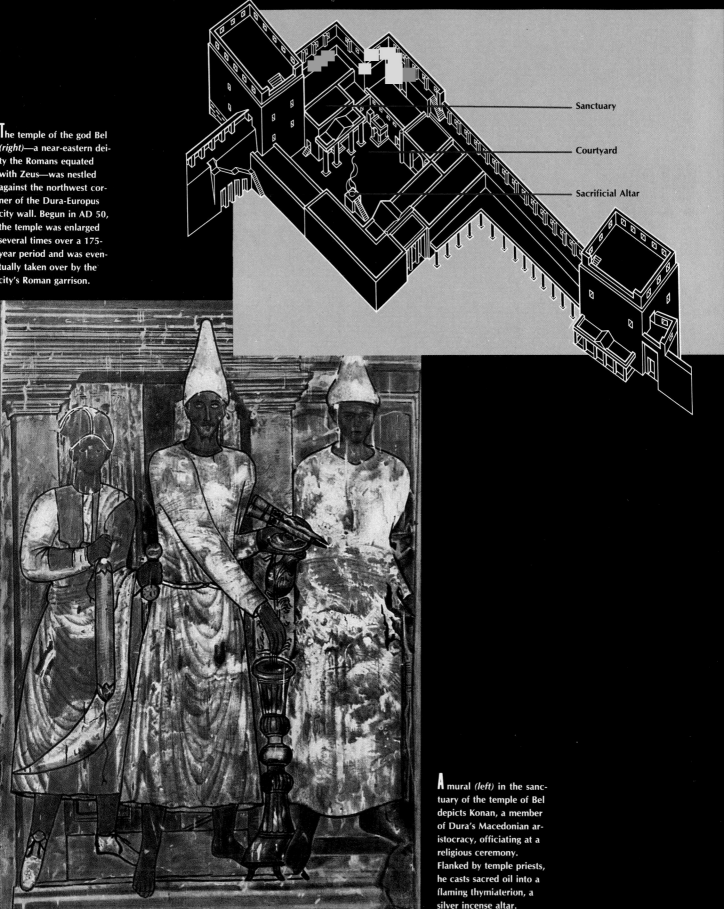

The temple of the god Bel *(right)*—a near-eastern deity the Romans equated with Zeus—was nestled against the northwest corner of the Dura-Europus city wall. Begun in AD 50, the temple was enlarged several times over a 175-year period and was eventually taken over by the city's Roman garrison.

Sanctuary

Courtyard

Sacrificial Altar

A mural *(left)* in the sanctuary of the temple of Bel depicts Konan, a member of Dura's Macedonian aristocracy, officiating at a religious ceremony. Flanked by temple priests, he casts sacred oil into a flaming thymiaterion, a silver incense altar.

In AD 245 a new Jewish synagogue was constructed in Dura-Europus *(right)*, replacing an earlier one that had stood on the site for over fifty years. Although the city's Jewish population was not large, Jews played a prominent role in the community and seem to have escaped persecution at the hands of the Roman garrison.

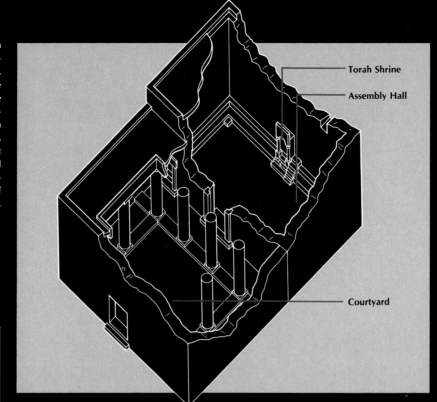

Torah Shrine

Assembly Hall

Courtyard

At the synagogue's heart was a painted Torah shrine *(below)*. The Biblical vignettes above its arch include the Temple in Jerusalem and Abraham's sacrifice of Isaac.

The assembly-hall walls in the Dura-Europus synagogue were decorated with Old Testament stories, including Moses' life. In the scene at right, Pharaoh's daughter saves the infant Moses from the Nile and hands the child to his mother and sister.

alienating even non-Christian Romans. From his deathbed, Galerius issued a proc-lamation ending the persecution—and pleading with Christians to pray for his sal-vation. Five days later, he died.

At the time of Galerius's death, the Roman Empire was already torn by civil strife. Scarcely had Diocletian and Maximian stepped aside on May 1, 305, than it became evident that the tetrarchy had been held together only by the strength of Diocletian's character. When the succeeding team was named, it failed to include as caesar an ambitious son of Constantius, Galerius's partner in the west: The rules of the tetrarchy specifically forbade hereditary succession. But that, as events would shortly demon-strate, was a mistake.

The young man's name was Constantine, and he was the issue of an early union between Constantius and one Helena, a woman of low birth from Bithynia. When Constantius, as part of the bargain by which he became a caesar, was required to abandon Helena and marry a daughter of Maximian, he nonetheless kept a paternal eye on Constantine, who remained in the east as one of Galerius's officers fighting the Persians. In fact, Galerius and Constantius distrusted each other, and the son was used as something of a hostage by Galerius to ensure the father's cooperation. Quite naturally, this grated on both Constantius and Constantine.

Now, as co-emperor, Constantius demanded the return of his son. Unless he wished a civil war, Galerius could scarcely refuse; Constantine swiftly made his way to Britain, where his father was fending off new barbarian assaults. There, the son distinguished himself in battle, and when Constantius died in York in 306, the army acclaimed Constantine as sole emperor, thereby opening the way to nearly two decades of sporadic civil war as Constantine sought to make good his title.

It was during this time that Constantine was transformed by a religious vision. As the story was told, Constantine was preparing for a crucial battle in 312 at Milvian Bridge near Rome when he saw a cross illuminated against the sun, accompanied by the words *in hoc signo vinces*—through this sign you will conquer. The next night, Christ appeared to Constantine in a dream and explained the meaning of the phe-nomenon: His men should enter into battle with the sign of Christ emblazoned on their shields. The night before the battle, Christ appeared again with the same mes-sage. The soldiers fought under the Christian sign; they won—and, although his formal conversion would not occur for a long time afterward, Constantine was ever after a friend to Christianity.

It was not until the summer of 324, after a bloody battle at Adrianople, that Constantine finally succeeded in his quest and became master of the Roman Empire. Upon becoming emperor, Constantine appointed Christians to high posts in his administration and formed a council of senior bishops to advise him on ecclesiastical matters, in which he took an intense and active interest.

As it happened, the empire's Christian community, for all its staunch appearance of unity under the fearful pressures of persecution, was by now bitterly divided over questions of doctrine. At the center of the storm in the east was a doctrine espoused by Arius, a priest trained at Antioch but serving in Alexandria, who denied the consubstantial existence of God the Father and God the Son, arguing that God was the ultimate deity who had created Jesus and was therefore superior to him. To settle the matter, Constantine in 325 summoned Christian bishops from throughout the empire to meet in ecumenical council at the Asian city of Nicaea.

More than 250 bishops answered the summons. With Constantine guiding their deliberations and urging an end to dissension, the bishops arrived at an orthodox creed, later known as the Nicene Creed. The doctrine held that God and Jesus were essentially the same spirit. All save Arius and two supporters signed the creed. To his relief, Constantine had at least temporarily effected a reunification of the church.

At about the same time, the emperor embarked upon a momentous project that would forever change the face and the fabric of his realm. It had long been recognized that the city of Rome was an anachronism as the empire's capital, and Constantine resolved to create a new capital of surpassing grandeur. And so it came to pass that the Roman emperor, spear in hand, paced out the perimeter of the city he meant to raise atop the ancient Greek trading town of Byzantium, situated on a Thracian promontory whose shores were bathed to the south by the Sea of Marmora, to the north by the waters of the Golden Horn, and to the east by the slender strand of the Bosphorus. On and on he strode, until at last, it was said, a weary member of his entourage asked how long he meant to continue. Replied Constantine the Great, who had a gift for visions that imparted a divine aura to his undertakings: "I shall go on until He who is walking in front of me stops."

With or without godly assistance, Constantine had chosen his site wisely. Not only did his Nova Roma—or, as it would soon come to be called, Constantinople—stand astride the main crossroads of world commerce, it more importantly offered easy access both to the emperor's western armies along the Danube and to his eastern forces facing Persia.

Never a patient man, Constantine pushed work at a frantic pace. Architects and artisans were summoned from the far reaches of Roman civilization; into the great harbor of the Golden Horn hove cargo ships laden with art treasures removed by imperial command from Rome, Athens, Antioch, and elsewhere in such quantities that one contemporary critic complained: "Almost every other city is stripped naked."

Like the empire's birthplace on the Tiber, Constantine's city was graced by seven hills, around whose slopes the emperor erected a hippodrome, a forum, and a senate house, along with a multitude of churches, law courts, and bathhouses, all enhanced by various gardens and groves that were watered by arched aqueducts.

Towering over all, atop a 100-foot-high shaft of red porphyry mounted on a 20-foot base of white marble, was a colossal gilt statue: its body was that of the pagan god Apollo upon which Constantine's head had been superimposed, and in one hand it held an orb that represented world power and supposedly contained a small piece of the True Cross.

Although the Roman Senate had long been in decline, Constantine still desired its presence and offered inducements for individual senators to move to the new city. When most of them rejected his offers, Constantine simply created a new senate for Constantinople.

By the reckoning of astrologers, May 11, 330, was deemed propitious for the dedication of the new city. On that date commenced forty days of games, circuses, and religious rites. In a clear sign that Constantine was not yet ready to sever ties to the old gods, pagan as well as Christian priests were permitted to offer prayers for the future prosperity of Constantinople and the greater glory of the Roman Empire.

During the remainder of his regime, Constantine paid homage to Christianity with

Seated atop a pillar, Saint Simeon the Stylite, one of many ascetics in the early Christian church, performs his devotions while ignoring the devil's temptations in this gold and silver icon. Simeon earned the name "Stylite"—from the Greek "stylo," or pillar—by spending the last thirty-six years of his life on a platform atop a column sixty feet tall near the Syrian town of Telanilssus. From his perch, Simeon converted many pilgrims, and in his honor a church and monastery were built on the spot after his death in 459—just as many early Christian edifices rose on sites where extraordinary acts of selflessness and piety occurred.

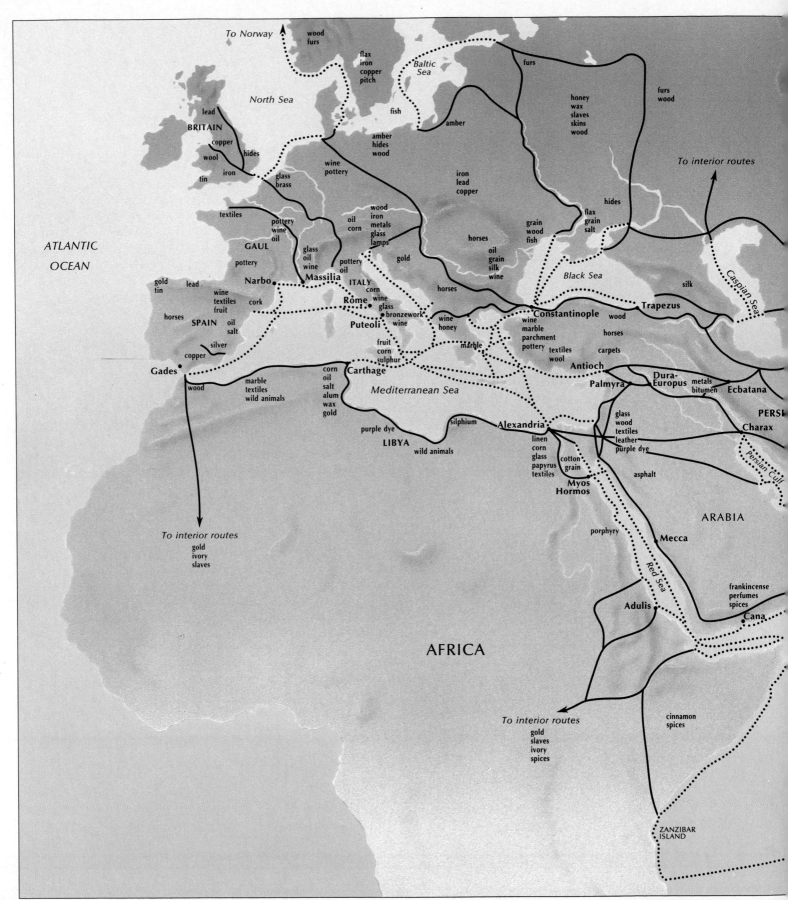

To Norway

wood
furs

flax
iron
copper
pitch

*Baltic
Sea*

furs

fish

amber

honey
wax
slaves
skins
wood

furs
wood

North Sea

amber
hides
wood

lead

BRITAIN

copper

wool
iron

tin

hides

glass
brass

wine
pottery

iron
lead
copper

hides

To interior routes

**ATLANTIC
OCEAN**

textiles

pottery
wine
oil

GAUL

pottery

glass
oil
wine

wood
iron
metals
glass
lamps

horses

oil
grain
silk
wine

flax
grain
salt

grain
wood
fish

To interior routes

silk

Caspian Sea

gold
tin

lead

wine
textiles
fruit

Narbo

cork

pottery
oil

Massilia

ITALY
corn
wine

Rome

glass

gold

horses

Black Sea

Constantinople

wood

Trapezus

silk

horses

SPAIN

oil
salt

bronzework
wine

Puteoli

wine
honey

wine
marble
parchment
pottery

textiles
wool

carpets

horses

silver

copper

fruit
corn
sulphur

marble

Antioch

Gades

wood

marble
textiles
wild animals

corn
oil
salt
alum
wax
gold

Carthage

Mediterranean Sea

Palmyra

**Dura-
Europus**

metals
bitumen

Ecbatana

glass
wood
textiles
leather
purple dye

PERSI

Charax

purple dye

silphium

Alexandria

linen
corn
glass
papyrus
textiles

cotton
grain

asphalt

Persian Gulf

LIBYA

wild animals

**Myos
Hormos**

ARABIA

porphyry

Mecca

frankincense
perfumes
spices

Adulis

Red Sea

Cana

To interior routes
gold
ivory
slaves

AFRICA

To interior routes
gold
slaves
ivory
spices

cinnamon
spices

**ZANZIBAR
ISLAND**

By the sixth century, routes of trade crisscrossed the ancient world, stitching together three continents and linking diverse cultures. At the heart of this network of sea-lanes, rivers, camel goods flowed into Constantinople's warehouses and workshops. Raw materials were either passed on to the West or made into finished items for home consumption or reexport.

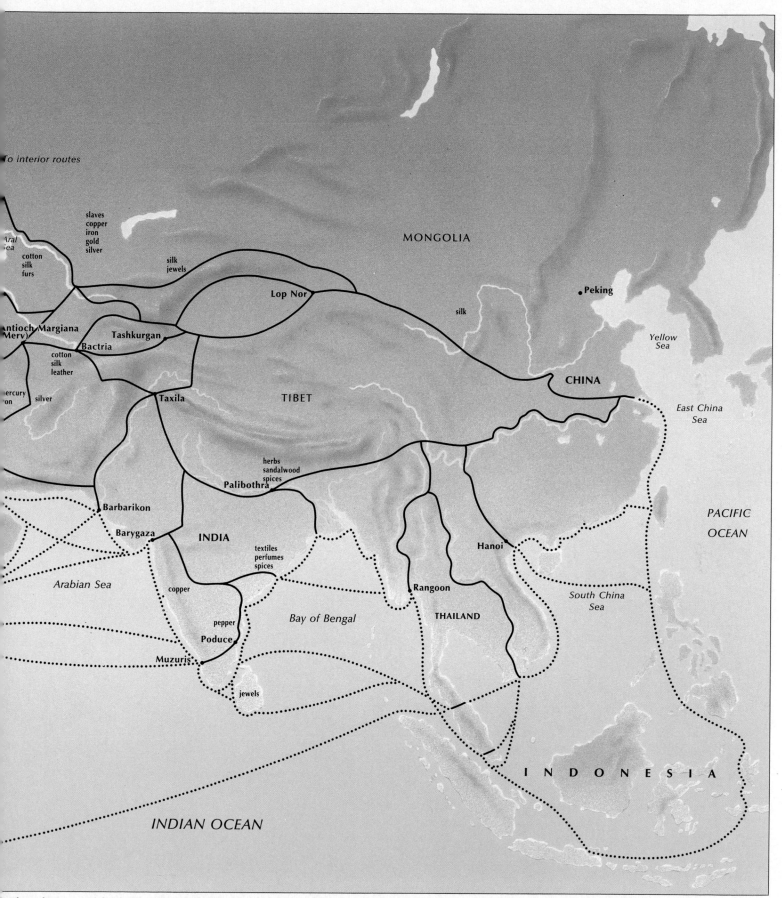

To interior routes

slaves
copper
iron
gold
silver

cotton
silk
furs

silk
jewels

MONGOLIA

Lop Nor

•Peking

ntioch Margiana
(Merv)

Tashkurgan

Bactria

cotton
silk
leather

silk

Yellow
Sea

ercury
on

silver

Taxila

TIBET

CHINA

East China
Sea

herbs
sandalwood
spices

Palibothra

Barbarikon

PACIFIC
OCEAN

Barygaza

INDIA

textiles
perfumes
spices

Hanoi

Arabian Sea

copper

Rangoon

South China
Sea

pepper

Bay of Bengal

THAILAND

Poduce

Muzuris

jewels

INDONESIA

INDIAN OCEAN

tracks, and Roman roads lay the city of Constantinople, the capital of eastern Rome and a bustling port of exchange. From as far away as Iceland, Ethiopia, northern Russia, Ceylon, and China, the construction of magnificent edifices—among them St. Peter's Basilica in Rome and the Church of the Holy Sepulcher, built in Jerusalem supposedly on the site where Christ had been buried.

But not until he lay on his deathbed in 337 was Constantine actually baptized in the faith to which he had contributed so much. As he received the sacraments, he is supposed to have said, "This is the moment for which I have hoped so long, craving for it and yearning to find salvation in God."

With the old emperor gone, the customary brutal struggle for power ensued. Constantine had left the empire to be divided among his three sons—Constantius, Constantinus, and Constans. Constantinus was felled in battle against Constans, who was later killed while fighting a would-be usurper. That left only one: Constantius, who survived until 361, when he died during preparations for battle with a cousin who had turned against him.

Fortunately for the empire, conditions during that period of internecine strife had been relatively tranquil along the borders, especially on the lower Danube, where the powerful Visigoths still observed a peace treaty signed with the emperor Constantine. In fact, along most of the empire's boundaries, a strange metamorphosis was taking place as barbarians became more romanized and Roman soldiers adopted the cultures of the border peoples.

Although small barbarian raids continued, they were accepted as part of life on the frontier, and they had little effect on exchanges that were now commonplace. In towns along the borders, Romans and barbarians mingled while traders peddled their wares. The barbarians favored trinkets, farm tools, wine and beer, along with wheat, which they had come to prefer over their traditional barley for making bread. In return, the tribesmen offered mainly slaves, taken in raids against other barbarians. Out of daily contact emerged shared styles: for example, it became faddish on both sides of the river to wear clasps and belt buckles fashioned by a faceting process that made them glitter and gleam in the sun. With the growth of frontier towns around garrisons, intermarriage was inevitable. And as time went on, Romans and barbarians developed a sort of composite culture while retaining their own enriched languages.

The Roman army was also a melting pot that offered thousands of barbarians employment both in its ranks and as workers in its camps. Indeed, the day was not too distant when barbarians would constitute a majority of the empire's soldiery, going into battle under Germanic commanders alongside Roman citizens who had adopted the barbarian costume of hide breeches and yowled their war cries as loudly and ferociously as any tribesman.

Perhaps most influential of all in drawing the cultures together was the coming of Christianity to the barbarians. Although the religion had found scattered and tenuous acceptance among the Visigoths on the Danube as early as 325, its development was greatly furthered by the mission of a remarkable man named Ulfila. Apparently the descendant of a Cappadocian family that had been taken captive in a Gothic raid into Asia Minor, Ulfila had been raised as a Visigoth, and it was as a member of a Gothic delegation that he had been sent to the Roman court in Constantinople. There he fell under the influence of the Arian bishop Eusebius of Nicomedia, who consecrated Ulfila as bishop to serve Christians among the Goths.

Swiftly gaining converts among a people always receptive to the beguiling ways of Roman civilization, Ulfila also provided the Goths with their first literature—a translation of the Bible (carefully edited, it was said, so as to omit certain Old Testament passages that might arouse warlike instincts among the tribesmen). To accomplish that mammoth task, the zealous bishop even invented an alphabet, derived from the Greek but with additional letters to accommodate Germanic sounds.

It was only natural that Ulfila's endeavors should meet with resistance from tribal chieftains who still adhered to the old gods, and in 348, after seven years of carrying the Gospel to the Goths, Ulfila was forced to seek refuge in Roman territory south of the Danube. He had, however, accomplished his mission: Not only had Christianity gained a firm foothold among the Visigoths, but it swiftly spread to other Germanic groups, among them the Vandals and the Burgundians.

The peace that had fallen upon the borders was too fragile to endure, and by the early 370s Roman commanders were reporting violent agitations in the barbarian realms beyond the empire's riverine borders. Fierce nomadic horsemen from the Eurasian interior were about to launch a migratory surge that would eventually engulf the western reaches of the empire.

East of the Volga River, bands of barbarians belonging to the Ural-Altaian (sometimes called Mongolian) race had long roamed the measureless steppes of Central Asia, camping for as long as the land could sustain their families, their horses, their herds, and their flocks, then moving on. To both the Romans and the Germans who later encountered them, the nomads were repulsive in their appearance and atrocious in their habits. "They all have stumpy, powerful legs and a muscular neck," wrote the Roman soldier-historian Ammianus, "but are so disfigured and bent that they could be taken for two-legged beasts. They have become so hardened by their way of life that they need no fire or seasoned food but live on the roots of wild plants or the half-raw meat of any animal."

Illiterate and so filthy that they customarily wore the same clothing until it rotted away, the nomads were comfortable only on horseback. "They are no good at all fighting on foot," Ammianus continued, "but are perfectly at home on their tough, ugly horses, which they sometimes ride sidesaddle when they relieve themselves. It is on horseback that each one of this people buys and sells, eats and drinks, and bent across the narrow neck of his steed, takes a deep sleep." They were also the "most fearful of all warriors"—highly mobile fighters who were deadly bowmen and, in closer combat, entangled the enemy with braided lassos and "fought man against man without regard to their own life."

From the Asian steppes those nomadic bands trekked slowly westward until at last they halted in the region east of the Caspian Sea. Soon after AD 370, however, they again restlessly began to move—and now they rode under the name by which they would become infamous throughout both the barbarian and Roman worlds and into the centuries to come: They were the Huns.

Their first victims were the Alans, a nomadic people of partly Iranian stock who had taken up residence in southern Russia east of the Don River. The Romans had found

Deep-draught trading vessels with cargoes destined for Rome unloaded at Ostia, a harbor constructed at the mouth of the Tiber River some fifteen miles southwest of the capital city. The ship in the relief shown here sails past Ostia's lighthouse and heroic statues of Neptune and other deities. In the third century AD, the harbor at Ostia silted up and shipping was diverted two miles up the coast to Portus, which was connected to the Tiber, and thence to Rome by canals.

the Alans to be particularly worthy warriors. But the fierce Huns conquered and subjugated them and then moved against another formidable foe: the Ostrogoths, who had established themselves in a kingdom extending from the Pripet Marshes south to the Black Sea and westward from the Don to the Dniester River.

Although horrifying reports of their cruelties had preceded the Huns, the elderly Ostrogothic king Ermanaric courageously gathered his warriors and for a time withstood the onrushing horde. Soon, however, it became all too evident that the Ostrogoths were outmatched. In despair, Ermanaric took his own life, and, while some of his subjects fled for refuge among their near kindred, the Visigoths, by far the larger part of the Ostrogothic tribesmen submitted to the loathsome invaders.

Next the Huns bore down on the Visigoths, whose chieftain Athanaric prepared to make a stand on the banks of the Dniester, meanwhile sending ahead a large force to scout the Hunnish approach. Easily evading the advance party, the Huns galloped through a moonlit night, crossed the Dniester, and fell upon Athanaric from the rear, taking him completely by surprise and sending his warriors in headlong flight for the Carpathian foothills. Shortly thereafter 200,000 Visigothic men, women, and children thronged the banks of the Danube, beseeching admittance to the Roman Empire to escape the Hunnish scourge.

After due consideration, Valens, then co-Augustus with responsibility for the eastern part of the empire, agreed to let the Visigoths settle south of the Danube in Moesia (modern Bulgaria). Valens shrewdly calculated that the barbarians would make valuable recruits for his army. And in any case, he lacked the border guards to halt a mass infiltration across the frozen Danube in winter.

But the alliance was an uneasy one from the outset. The Visigoths were anything but docile, and the mistrustful Romans deprived them of their cherished weapons. Worse, the new settlers were ceded the poorest agricultural lands; they had to purchase grain that was often rotten and priced outrageously by venal Roman functionaries. So cruelly arbitrary was the Roman rule that on one occasion a Roman official invited two Visigothic leaders to his home and as they were dining, he had one of the chieftains slain along with the Goth personal guards.

The reaction to the situation was violent. In 378, scarcely two years after their crossing of the Danube, the Visigoths rose furiously in revolt and went rampaging not only across Moesia but into neighboring provinces as well. Marching to suppress them, Valens and his army found the barbarians' encampment near Adrianople, about 100 miles northwest of Constantinople, and immediately attacked. Unfortunately for the emperor, most of the Visigoth warriors were out foraging at the time; returning while the assault was still in progress, the horsemen formed ranks and hurled themselves at the Roman left, wrote a contemporary historian, "like a thunderbolt that strikes upon a mountaintop and dashes away all that stands in its path." When quiet at last descended upon the battlefield, Valens was dead and two-thirds of his mobile field army, the elite of Rome's eastern forces, had been annihilated.

Selected to replace Valens as co-Augustus in the east was one Theodosius, a former military governor in Moesia and the son of a renowned general. After several years of inconclusive fighting, Theodosius wisely made peace with the Visigoths, paying them subsidies and granting them lands in northern Greece; in return, the Visigoths undertook to defend the lower Danube against encroachment by other barbarians.

As an ardent Christian, Theodosius promulgated laws that abolished pagan sacrifice and shut down the heathen temples. Yet for all his religious involvement, Emperor Theodosius suffered his greatest humiliation at the hands of the Church.

One episode grew out of a brief and abortive uprising in 390 against Roman authority in the Illyrian city of Thessalonica, in reprisal for which Theodosius ordered the massacre of 7,000 citizens. As punishment for that most unchristian act, Bishop Ambrose of Milan required that Theodosius, upon threat of excommunication, do public penance. And so it occurred that Milan's Christian congregation witnessed the astonishing spectacle of a Roman emperor, stripped of his imperial insignia, appearing in church and begging forgiveness for the sin of Thessalonica.

Theodosius's penance was dramatic evidence of the great strides made by the Christian church since Constantine had elevated it to respectability. To be sure, the Church was still plagued by schism. The religious unity that Constantine attempted to impose at Nicaea lasted no longer than his reign. By the time of Theodosius, most Christians were split along regional lines over the question of doctrine, with the Greek-speaking east generally favoring Arianism while the Latin speakers of the west adhered to the "orthodox" view. Among barbarian Christians, it was Arianism that won the most advocates, despite virulent efforts by Theodosius to supress the doctrine. Yet the Christian church of the late fourth century, enlivened by embryonic forms of the art and architecture that would flourish in a future age, enhanced by a flowering literature, and inspired by the brilliance of its theological thinkers, had steadily ascended toward a position of supremacy in the religious world of the Roman Empire.

In the structure of their religious edifices, Christians were confronted by practical considerations: The ritual of the Eucharist called for simple, spacious interiors in which the faithful could celebrate their communion. Thus, Christians turned to a conventional Roman secular form: the basilica. And by the end of the century they had widely adopted it, with its nave, side aisles, and illuminated clerestories. It was an edifice that seemed comfortably Christian and one that presaged the great cathedrals of the medieval west.

The struggles of the new Christian culture to transform or discard its secular Greco-Roman roots were reflected in its writings. The great scholar and ecclesiastical historian Eusebius sought to demonstrate how superior the Bible was to classical philosophy and history, yet he freely acknowledged their vital role in paving the way for Christianity. For all the Christian ardor of his religious poems, Paulinus of Nola could never escape his classical heritage, while from the redoubtable Bishop Ambrose came sermons, hymns, Biblical commentaries, and treatises that mirrored Ciceronian rhetoric along with a thorough knowledge of Greek philosophy. Yet among them all, the one who would make the most enduring mark was the acidulous Jerome of Dalmatia, whose superb translation of the Bible into Latin would come to be known as the Vulgate and would survive as the scriptural text of the modern Roman Catholic church.

In the realm of theological thought, Gregory of Nazianzus, Basil of Caesarea, and Basil's brother, Gregory of Nyssa, were towering figures in the Greek east, while few in the Latin west compared with the great Augustine. Born in Numidia of a pagan father and raised as a Christian by a Christian mother, Augustine was educated in Carthage, where he lived freely enough to sire a bastard son. He shortly turned to more intellectual matters, and in his unending quest for universal meaning, Augustine tested such doctrines as Skepticism, Neoplatonism, and for nine years, Manichaeism. He found them all wanting, but it was not until the age of thirty-two, when as a

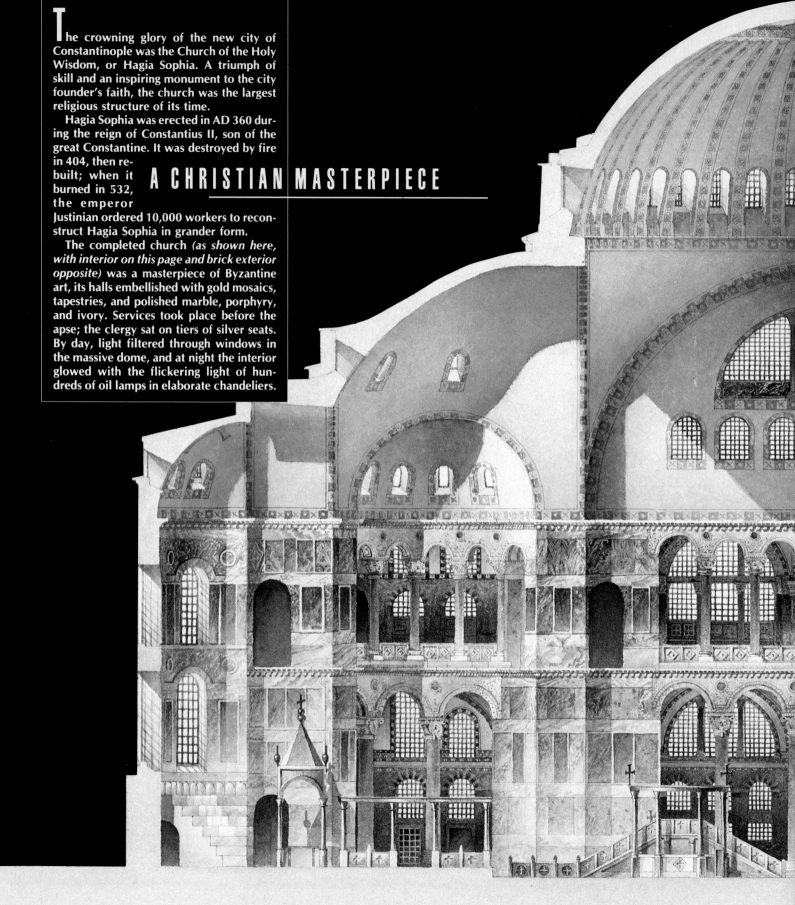

The crowning glory of the new city of Constantinople was the Church of the Holy Wisdom, or Hagia Sophia. A triumph of skill and an inspiring monument to the city founder's faith, the church was the largest religious structure of its time.

Hagia Sophia was erected in AD 360 during the reign of Constantius II, son of the great Constantine. It was destroyed by fire in 404, then rebuilt; when it burned in 532, the emperor Justinian ordered 10,000 workers to reconstruct Hagia Sophia in grander form.

A CHRISTIAN MASTERPIECE

The completed church *(as shown here, with interior on this page and brick exterior opposite)* was a masterpiece of Byzantine art, its halls embellished with gold mosaics, tapestries, and polished marble, porphyry, and ivory. Services took place before the apse; the clergy sat on tiers of silver seats. By day, light filtered through windows in the massive dome, and at night the interior glowed with the flickering light of hundreds of oil lamps in elaborate chandeliers.

APSE — ALTAR

0   50   100

SCALE IN FEET

The dome of Hagia Sophia was 100 feet in diameter and 200 feet high. Four piers of limestone bore the weight of the masonry.

professor of rhetoric at Milan he came under the influence of Bishop Ambrose, that Augustine again fully embraced Christianity.

In his extraordinary ability to blend Platonic mysticism with Christian faith, and in his compelling view of humanity as fallen creatures subject only to the grace of God, Augustine reached out to the mind as well as the spirit. "We could not even believe," he wrote, "unless we possessed rational souls."

The emperor Theodosius reigned for sixteen years and upon his death in AD 395 bequeathed the empire to his two young sons: One, Arcadius, eighteen years old, was to rule in the east, while the younger, Honorius, scarcely ten, would reign in the west. Although some Romans continued to regard the two regions as parts of a single empire, the division was in fact a permanent condition that acted to the vast disadvantage of the beleaguered west, which could no longer rely on the stronger, more affluent east for material resources or military assistance.

As matters evolved, neither Arcadius nor Honorius proved equal to his heritage. Arcadius was co-emperor only nominally. His ministers actually ruled. Honorius, a child, could do no better. In 402, when Milan was menaced by marauding barbarians, the boy emperor's capital was hurriedly moved to Ravenna, an Adriatic port protected on its inland side by a maze of marshes, sodden flats, and small streams. There, Honorius spent much of his reign in seclusion, so aloof from his people and their affairs that a later historian claimed he was familiar with "Roma" only as the name of his pet chicken.

For the first decade or so of Honorius's rule, the defense of his empire was, by Theodosius's last request, entrusted to a general who was half Vandal. The soldier's name was Stilicho. He had risen to high rank under Theodosius, and in the service of Honorius he performed as best he could. The Visigoths, dissatisfied with the lands Theodosius had granted them, streamed out of the Balkans and invaded the empire's Italian homeland. Stilicho fended them off, only to face another devastating invasion from beyond the Danube. To meet these extraordinary threats, he may have been compelled to call for reinforcements from the legions defending the Rhine. If he did so, it was a calamitous error. For on the bitterly cold night of December 31, 406, there was apparently no Roman army on guard when a host of Vandal, Alan, Suevi, and Burgundian warriors, along with women, children, and possessions, streamed across the frozen Rhine and headed southwest through Gaul. This time, the frontiers of the Roman Empire had been breached by barbarians who meant to stay.

Still, Stilicho might eventually have repaired the damage had not the brooding Honorius suddenly committed an astonishing mistake. In 408, apparently fearing that Stilicho and his allies were attempting to seize imperial power, he ordered his faithful general executed—thereby unwittingly opening the way for an enemy Visigoth chieftain whom Stilicho had frequently frustrated.

The chieftain was called Alaric, and he was a man to be reckoned with. In the past, he had repeatedly raided in Italy and the Balkans only to be driven back by Stilicho. Now, with Stilicho removed, Alaric led his warriors against Rome, laying the city under siege and departing only after authorities had bowed to his demands for an immense tribute that included 5,000 pounds of gold and 30,000 pounds of silver.

Two years later, in 410, Alaric was back again, his force bolstered by thousands of resident Italian barbarians. This time, apparently assisted by sympathizers from within the city, the Visigoths swarmed into Rome and spent three raucous days gathering up all the movable treasures their horses could carry or pull. Although Alaric left the city itself largely intact, the significance of his incursion was enormous: For the first time since 390 BC, when Rome had been looted by Gauls, the ancient capital had been in the hands of a barbarian horde—and the apparent helplessness of the imperial regime offered encouragement to enemies on all the frontiers of the western empire.

A few months later, Alaric died in southern Italy while still seeking a homeland for his people. His place was taken by his brother-in-law, a shrewd leader named Ataulf, who hoped to accomplish by diplomacy what Alaric had failed to achieve by force. Seeking alliance with Rome, he petitioned Honorius for permission to wed the emperor's sister Galla Placidia, who had been taken as hostage during Alaric's assault on Rome. Honorius, forever foolish, haughtily rejected the proposal—whereupon Ataulf went right ahead and married the woman, who was entirely willing.

Even a year and a half later, Honorius had still not accepted his brother-in-law as an ally. At this point, Ataulf was murdered by one his own servants. His place as leader of the Visigoths was taken by Vallia, who returned Placidia to the Romans and further demonstrated his loyalty to Rome by campaigning vigorously against barbarians who had invaded Spain. For their services, the Visigoths were at last awarded a fertile homeland in southwestern Gaul, where they established the kingdom of Toulouse—the first barbarian state on imperial land. From Toulouse, they eventually expanded into Spain, dispossessing Vandals who had settled there in the years since crossing the Rhine in 406.

After that fateful crossing, the Vandals had smashed through Gaul and in their passage had left a wake that would make their name a synonym for wanton destruction. Wrote Orientius, a Roman bishop and poet: "See how swiftly death comes upon the world and how many peoples the violence of war has stricken. Some lay as food for the dogs; others were killed by the flames that licked their homes. In the villages and country houses, in the fields and in the countryside, on every road—death, sorrow, slaughter, fires, and lamentation. All Gaul smoked in one great funeral pyre."

By 409 the Vandals had passed over the Pyrenees and into Spain, where they remained until pressures from the increasingly powerful Visigoths became intolerable. Then, confronted by a choice between fighting the Visigoths or departing, they determined to move. To lead them, they chose a crippled genius named Gaiseric, said to be the son of a slave, as cunning as he was cruel, who would cause untold harm and havoc to the Roman Empire of the west.

In 429, Gaiseric and his entire people—80,000 Vandals and allies, of whom no more than 15,000 could be counted as warriors—crossed the Strait of Gibraltar and landed in North Africa, probably near Tangiers. Of all its holdings, the western Roman Empire could probably least afford to lose North Africa, whose bountiful granary was vital to Rome, still an exceptionally large city with heavy demands for food. But lose it they did. The Vandals moved irresistibly eastward along the North African coast, capturing one city after another—among them Hippo, whose venerable Bishop Augustine perished of fever during a year-long siege. Finally, in 439, Carthage fell virtually undefended, and Gaiseric established a Vandal kingdom dedicated to exploitation at home and continued expansion and piracy abroad. In no small measure, his success rested on his ability to strike swiftly from the sea; he was the first barbarian king to build a fleet, and this gave him great mobility and power.

Even while retaining Roman functionaries to perform certain administrative tasks,

Gaiseric took over many Roman estates in order to support his warriors; the former landowners were, like the Roman orthodox clergy, put to hard labor. And as a zealous follower of Arianism, Gaiseric enriched both his faith and himself by confiscating Roman property.

Gaiseric won Roman recognition of his despotic kingdom in 442. The pragmatic Romans hoped to buy him off, to no avail. Making and breaking treaties with equal disregard for diplomatic amenities, the Vandal lord seized Corsica, Sardinia, and Sicily and used them as bases for a profitable piratical enterprise against the coasts of Spain, Greece, and Italy. In 455, he undertook yet another plundering of Rome. In recognizing the Vandal kingdom in Africa, Rome had apparently acted upon the urging of another strongman who, like Stilicho before him, had assumed control of the western empire while an indolent monarch ruled in name only. The new leader was Aetius, a Roman patrician who had in his youth experienced life as a hostage among both the Visigoths and the Huns, whose warlike ways he had come to admire; indeed, he had maintained close relations with the Huns, and this was to become an important source of power.

By now a successful general, Aetius was perfectly willing to sacrifice Africa in order to preserve Gaul for the empire. This chiefly meant controlling barbarian confederates in Gaul and keeping them within the limits of their allotted lands. To accomplish that aim, Aetius would stop at nothing. In the late 420s, pitting barbarian against barbarian, he unleashed in his cause the terrible force of the Huns, whose great leader Attila would soon inspire dread in the hearts of all those who stood in his path.

For a number of decades, the Romans had made use of the Huns as reliable auxiliaries, to keep other peoples in check. Quite naturally, this arrangement had built up Hunnish resources and confidence and had opened the way for a leader such as Attila, who meant to exercise ambitions of his own.

As later described by the historian Priscus, Attila was a squat, heavy-shouldered man with a flat nose and a few wispy facial hairs that stood for a beard. Priscus wrote that Attila's dark, deep-set eyes softened only as he stroked the cheek of a young son; otherwise they were as cold and unreadable as obsidian.

According to the historian, who had accompanied a diplomatic mission to the Hunnish headquarters on the Hungarian plain, Attila's encampment was a rude collection of wood, mud, and straw huts, with a number of wooden watchtowers overlooking the smoky, noisy scene. Attila and his retinue dwelled in a somewhat more elaborate compound constructed of polished wood. But the only imposing building in the camp was a curious stone bathhouse that had been built by a captured Roman architect, who was then kept as a slave to serve as the bath's attendant.

When returning to the village from an excursion, Attila was escorted by singing handmaidens and provided with food and a goblet of wine, which he consumed while still mounted before riding to his quarters. Such was Attila's power that in his rude camp he received emissaries from many nations.

Clearly, these were no barbarians to trifle with, and Aetius would one day rue his employment of the Huns. For the time being, however, they performed their assignments with bloody efficiency. In 437, they fell murderously on the Burgundians, a Germanic tribe that had crossed the Rhine in 406 with the Vandals and

A mosaic in the great church of Hagia Sophia commemorates the religious devotion and the temporal achievements of Constantine and Justinian, rulers of the eastern empire, whose energy and resolve created many awe-inspiring monuments to the Christian faith. Both of the emperors are shown in the act of dedicating symbolic gifts to the Virgin and infant Jesus; Constantine *(right)* bestows the walled city of Constantinople, while Justinian presents Hagia Sophia itself.

had recently incurred Aetius's displeasure by expanding along the river's west bank.

The Burgundians, however, were good soldiers, even in defeat, and Aetius had a use for them. Rather than permitting the Huns to annihilate the Burgundians, Aetius allowed them to settle in the area of Geneva, where they accepted federate status and were henceforth available for service with Roman armies. Toward the end of the fifth century, the Burgundians would expand their holdings from Geneva to Lyon and establish a kingdom extending from southern Champagne to the Durance River and the Maritime Alps.

As for the Huns, the campaigns undertaken at Aetius's behest had only whetted their thirst for plunder. By now, Attila had risen to vicious prominence—after murdering his brother Bleda—and he turned his attentions to the Roman Empire itself, judiciously selecting the eastern realm as his objective. In 443, he drove deep into the Balkans. There he left Naissus, the birthplace of Constantine the Great, in smouldering ruins, pillaged Sardica (modern Sofia), and galloped down the military highway leading to Constantinople, turning back only when the eastern emperor offered him a tribute of 6,000 pounds of gold and an annual subsidy of 2,100 pounds.

Four years later, Attila and his Huns returned, and this time they found the eastern empire already in desperate condition. For four months, a series of earthquakes had devastated the region, swallowing up entire villages, leveling hillocks, and burying thousands of citizens beneath the rubble of collapsed buildings.

In the aftermath of the earthquakes, plague swept through Constantinople, killing thousands more. And then came the Huns, ravaging the countryside on their way to the city. "There were so many murders and bloodlettings," wrote the Roman Callinicus, "that the dead could not be numbered. Aye, for they took captive the churches and monasteries and slew the monks and maidens in great numbers."

This time the Huns were met by a Roman army, commanded by a Goth, Arnegisclus, who put up a stubborn fight before he was killed and his legions put to rout. But after the battle, Attila did not press his advantage; the Huns had apparently suffered severe losses of their own, and Attila was perhaps fearful of plague spreading among his men. In any case, he called a halt and later withdrew—but only after exacting another immense tribute.

Now the Huns turned their rapacious eyes westward. Attila may well have been dismayed by the stout resistance he had encountered in the east, and although the western empire could offer much less in the way of loot, it also figured to be easier prey. Attila therefore decided on an invasion of Gaul, and to justify the deed he hit upon a bizarre excuse.

It seemed that the lady Honoria, a sister of the western emperor Valentinian III, had been discovered in a love affair with a palace steward. The unfortunate steward had been immediately executed, and the disgraced Honoria was ordered to marry a wealthy but boring senator. Rather than accept that dreary fate, Honoria dispatched to Attila a servant named Hyacinth, offering a bribe to the warlord if he would rescue her from her dilemma. To prove the authenticity of the message, Hyacinth showed Attila a ring belonging to Honoria—which the Hun took for a proposal of marriage. He thereupon demanded the delivery of his betrothed, along with half the territory of the western empire for a dowry. When Valentinian refused, Attila declared war.

In the spring of 451, Attila marched into Gaul at the head of his Huns and accompanied by a mighty array of Germanic vassals—among them Ostrogoths, Gepids, Thuringians, Sciri, Rugians, and Heruli. To meet them, the Roman general

Aetius had arranged with great difficulty to round up an assortment of Franks, Saxons, Burgundians, Celts, and even his old foes the Visigoths, who joined to protect their own kingdom from the Huns. The opposing armies came together near Troyes, about 130 miles southeast of Paris on the Catalaunian plain, and for a full day they struggled. Wrote a sixth-century historian: "Hand to hand they clashed in battle, and the fight grew fierce, confused, monstrous, unrelenting." When it was over, both sides were exhausted, and there was no clear winner. But Attila had had enough, and he shortly withdrew across the Rhine.

Two years later, while contemplating a new attack on the Roman east, Attila married a German woman named Ildico. On his wedding night, while exerting himself in the bridal chamber, Attila ruptured a blood vessel and died. As for the Roman Aetius, he ran afoul of the jealous and insecure emperor Valentinian, who staged a quarrel while they were discussing imperial accounts. Aided by a palace eunuch, Valentinian hacked Aetius to death with a sword. Shortly thereafter, Valentinian himself was assassinated by the personal bodyguards of the lamented Aeitus.

The final decades of the Roman Empire in the west were now at hand. With the death of Valentinian in 455 there followed a giddy succession of claimants, pretenders, usurpers, and puppets, none of them capable of wielding imperial power. Vandal kings held sway in Spain and North Africa; Gaul had passed out of Roman control and was ruled by Burgundians, Bretons, and Franks. The western empire now consisted only of Italy and parts of two northern provinces, Raetia and Noricum. Even in that reduced realm, real power was exercised by barbarian generals, and on September 4, 476, one of them, a general Odoacer, deposed a fledgling emperor whose names ironically evoked both the legendary first king of the city of Rome and the father of the Roman Empire—Romulus Augustulus.

The usurpation signaled the end of the western empire. It was accomplished so casually that Odoacer did not even bother to murder the boy. Instead, he sent Romulus Augustulus off to a provincial villa, where he lived in contentment until well into the next century.

Although the emperor had been deposed, the government of Italy—both civil and military—remained largely unchanged, with the same Romans still holding traditional offices. Indeed, some Roman senators considered affairs so promising that they took the occasion to have their seats in the Colosseum refurbished.

Odoacer, who ruled as undisputed monarch of Italy, needed only recognition from the eastern empire, now under the emperor Zeno, to achieve legitimacy for his reign. Zeno, as it turned out, was considerably too clever for his own good. When Odoacer pledged to acknowledge the authority of the east, in exchange for recognition, Zeno seemed to agree. Yet as events would soon demonstrate, he was merely biding his time until he could pit his enemies against each other.

Zeno's scheme included the Ostrogoths. Freed from Hunnish subjugation after the death of Attila and the subsequent dissolution of his tribe, the Ostrogoths had settled in Macedonia, where they incurred imperial displeasure by incessantly making raids on their neighbors. Anxious to be permanently rid of them, Zeno sensed an opportunity to destroy two barbarian regimes with a single stroke. He therefore commissioned the Ostrogoth king Theodoric to invade Italy and oust Odoacer from power. If the opposing forces engaged in a battle of mutual extermination, so much the better. As for Theodoric, he was eager to comply with Zeno's request, if only because

The ascendancy of the Byzantine Empire inspired an artistic reawakening that altered the face of the Mediterranean world. And in no medium was the exotic grandeur of the eastern empire more eloquently expressed than in the art of the mosaic.

The creation of a mosaic *(below)* was a complicated procedure that called for careful timing and teamwork by a group of trained and experienced artisans. Since even small amounts of moisture could eventually destroy a mosaic, walls were painted with resin or tar before being covered with the first of three layers of plaster. The first coat, the foundation, contained sand and crushed brick in order to provide a good binding for the second and third layers, which were of finer consistency.

Sometimes nails would be driven into the wall to provide additional support. A sketch of the projected work was then made on the plaster to serve as a guide for the various artisans.

The outermost layer of plaster, in which the pieces, or tesserae, of the mosaic would be set, was spread on only enough area to contain a day's work. Some of the tesserae—small, carefully cut fragments of colored glass, marble, and semiprecious stones—were pressed into the wet plaster so that they projected at a slight angle. The stones thereby better reflected light and imbued the finished mosaic with a shimmering life of its own.

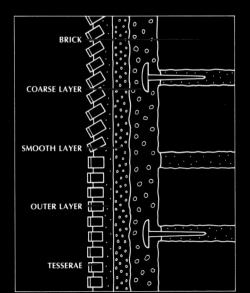

BRICK

COARSE LAYER

SMOOTH LAYER

OUTER LAYER

TESSERAE

mosaic *(above)* made in
D 547 at Ravenna's
hurch of San Vitale por-
ays the empress Theo-
dora and her attendants. A
detail *(right)* shows multicolored tesserae, including
mother-of-pearl, to denote
the lights and shadows of
the empress's face and to
create her halo and bejeweled crown.

his father had killed Odoacer's father in battle, and thus the sons were blood enemies.

The Ostrogoth army arrived in Italy in 489, but nearly four years of bitter fighting passed before Theodoric got the upper hand and forced Odoacer to withdraw into the forbidding defenses of the seacoast city Ravenna. There Odoacer withstood a lengthy siege and then wearily agreed to a compromise: He would surrender on condition that he and Theodoric share power in Italy. Entering Ravenna under a flag of truce, Theodoric swiftly and personally murdered Odoacer, while his men slaughtered the monarch's family and many of his officers. It was a bloody start for a reign that would generally be marked by a benign and civilized wisdom.

As a youth, Theodoric had been held hostage and educated in Constantinople, where he was thoroughly exposed to Roman culture and institutions. Now, as ruler of what remained of the old western empire, he sought to preserve the best of both the Roman and the barbarian worlds. "We rejoice in living under Roman law, which we hope to defend by force of arms," he said during a ceremonial visit to Rome. "Our ambition, with God's help, is to reap such victories that our subjects will regret not having placed themselves under our sovereignty sooner."

The result was a curious dualism in which Ostrogoths and Romans each existed under their own laws, unified only by the authority of the emperor. Roman officials were employed in their traditional functions, and from his capital at Ravenna, Theodoric embarked on an ambitious public-works program in a state that had become sadly dilapidated; roads were built, seaports renovated, aqueducts restored, and Ravenna and other cities embellished with stunning palaces and churches.

Theodoric also worked ceaselessly to forge close ties, sometimes reinforced by marriage, with Vandals, Franks, Burgundians, and Visigoths, all barbarian regimes like his own. Yet if Theodoric entertained notions of establishing a new western commonwealth to replace the old western empire, he was frustrated by the explosive ambitions of a tribal ruler in Gaul, where momentous events were taking place.

In a long and complex history, the Frankish tribes had fought fearsomely against the

Although geographically distorted, this Roman map was drawn to provide a traveler on the empire's roads with important information: the location of towns and the distance between them. Towns are denoted by the symbols that resemble buildings—the bigger the symbol, the larger the town—and mileage is indicated by Roman numerals. The thin, wavy line that stretches horizontally near the top of the map represents the Rhine River on the empire's frontier; at top left, nestled in a crook of the descending Moselle River, is the trading center of Trier. The thick, dark band in the lower half of the map is the Mediterranean Sea, with the coast of Africa beneath it. At far left is the port of Marseille; at far right, in the elongated sea, are Corsica and Sardinia.

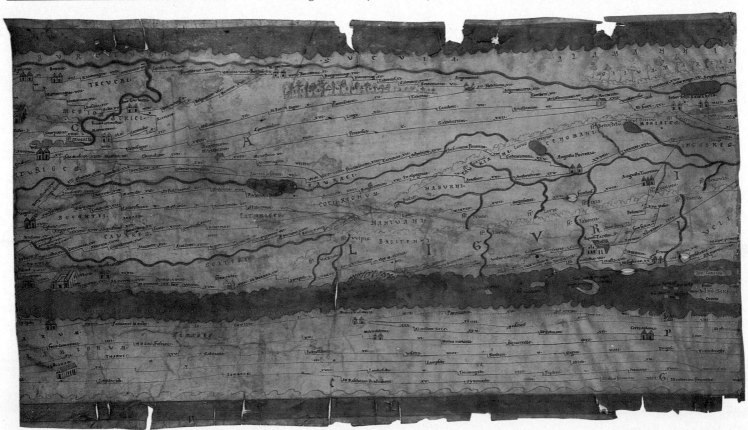

Roman legions, had been beaten down, and then had aligned themselves with Roman interests. In the early fourth century, they had settled in Belgium as confederates of Rome, and their subsequent expansion across the Rhine seems to have met with little Roman opposition. By the time of Theodoric's accession to power in Italy, the tribe had emerged as a powerful and cohesive people led by a king named Clovis.

As scion of the Merovingian line of chieftains, which took its name from his grandfather Merovech, Clovis had come to his throne in 481 at the age of fifteen and, while still in his early twenties, had proved his mettle by subjugating all of the cities north of the Loire as far as Burgundy and Brittany.

Clovis was a ruthless and inspired war leader and a keen though sometimes faithless diplomat who understood the contending forces at work in his world. Born and reared as a pagan, he recognized the advantages that might accrue to his ambitions if he were supported by the empire's Catholic church, whose bishops in Gaul he assiduously courted. The bishops returned the favor, and they liked Clovis even more when he took as his wife a Christian Burgundian princess, Clothilde.

In 496, amid all the ritual circumstance that Roman Christianity could provide, Clovis led thousands of his Frankish warriors to be baptized by the bishop Remigius at Rheims. From then on, Clovis and his Franks could claim to be the champions of the church in the war against barbarian Arianism. "Your faith is our triumph," wrote Bishop Avitus of Burgundian Vienne. "Every battle you fight is a victory for us."

Clovis overwhelmed the pagan Alamanni of Alsace, then turned against the Visigoths who dwelled beyond the Loire. "It grieves me," he said, "that these Arians should hold a part of Gaul." In 507, Clovis smashed the Visigoths in a battle near Poitiers, then drove them southward into Spain.

After his triumphal return, Clovis soon moved his capital from Soissons to a strategically located city on the Seine. Its name was Paris, and it would endure as a center of human civilization long after Clovis and his Franks had become but a dim memory in the mind of humanity.

When Clovis died in 511, his kingdom was divided among his four sons. Despite a number of vicious internecine disputes, they nonetheless extended the Frankish domain to Burgundy, Provence, and the territory of the Thuringians. The last remaining son of Clovis, Clothar, survived until 561, when he divided the kingdom among his own four feisty sons.

From Ravenna, Theodoric had observed the rise of the Franks with considerable unease, and at times he intervened to keep their ambitions from getting completely out of hand. Yet he concentrated mainly on the tricky task of holding together his own Italian kingdom of Romans and Ostrogoths. He maintained his grip for thirty-three years. But it was only a personal triumph, and the structure that he had built started to fall apart shortly after his death in 526.

With Theodoric gone, a fragile power was passed to his widowed daughter, Amalasuntha, acting as regent for her young son. All too aware that her position was precarious, Amalasuntha sought support from the newly installed emperor of the east, a forty-five-year-old Macedonian named Justinian, nephew of the emperor Justin I, an experienced leader. Justinian accepted the hand of friendship—and would one day use his amiable but remote relationship with Amalasuntha as the excuse for moving toward the fulfillment of a dream.

Justinian was an energetic and conscientious administrator who took a direct interest in the smallest details of responsibility. "The emperor never sleeps," said one

By the fourth century the city of Trier on the Moselle River in northern Gaul had evolved from a beleaguered military outpost into one of the most prosperous communities in the Roman the largest producer of gold and silver coins in the western empire. Trier was noted for its monumental architecture, including a forum, an amphitheater, and a massive bridge that spanne

Empire. Pacification of the region and the introduction of Christianity encouraged economic growth. The city was both an agricultural and a manufacturing center, and the Trier mint was ...he Moselle. Its schools—both Christian and pagan—were among the finest educational facilities in the empire.

of his functionaries. Yet he was at the same time capable of grand and sweeping concepts. Within two years after becoming emperor, he established a number of juridical commissions charged with nothing less than emending, recodifying, and imposing an orderly system upon the body of all previous Roman law. The result was the famed *Corpus Juris Civilis,* which would in future ages become the model for the legal system of nearly every European nation.

Among his other talents, Justinian had a gift for surrounding himself with the most capable people of his day—administrators, lawyers, architects (who rebuilt in all its lasting magnificence the church of Hagia Sophia in Constantinople), generals, and not least, his wife, Theodora.

She was an improbable consort, the daughter, said some malicious gossips, of a bear keeper at the Hippodrome in Constantinople, an actress and a courtesan who, after being abandoned by a lover in Alexandria, apparently determined to mend her ways. Back in Constantinople, she somehow attracted the attention of Justinian, who then had to persuade his uncle the emperor to amend the law so that he could marry a woman of such dubious background. For the rest of her life, Theodora would stand indomitably at the side of her husband, sustaining him through good times and bad.

From the outset of his reign, whether as a matter of high vision or of shrewd opportunism, Justinian set out to restore the Roman Empire to its ancient glories. The foes were formidable: Vandals ruled North Africa; the Franks held sway in Gaul and the Visigoths in Spain; Britain, long ago abandoned by the Romans, was by now under almost constant assault by the Germanic Saxons, who along with their Angle and Jute kindred would eventually take over the island; and Italy, the cradle of Roman civilization, was in the hands of the Ostrogoths.

Justinian remained undaunted. In 533, he sent his brilliant general Belisarius to North Africa at the head of 18,000 infantry and cavalry. With surprising ease, this force disposed of a Vandal nation grown soft and corrupt and wracked by revolt. Opportunity next presented itself in Italy, where Justinian found a righteous cause avenging the murder of his friend Amalasuntha by the evil cousin she had married and with whom she shared power after the death of her son. In 535, Belisarius and his army took ship for Italy, besieged and captured Naples, and marched into Rome after driving the Ostrogoths from the Eternal City. But then, when he was on the verge of victory, the Ostrogoths rallied, and nearly two decades of desperate fighting remained before their resistance was finally smashed.

Justinian's dream of empire was ended. For the rest of his life he would be diverted from his great goal by the need to defend his eastern borders against the aggressive Persians. The Italy he had set out to reconquer was destroyed, not liberated, its countryside scorched by years of war, many of its citizens massacred, others starving, its great cities—Rome, Naples, and Milan—all but deserted. In 565, the old emperor died, and within three years the Lombards, Germanic warriors who had helped Justinian put down the Ostrogoths, began the push that would enable them to become the rulers of northern Italy.

Although Constantinople, sustained by its version of orthodox Christianity, would survive and eventually flourish as the wellspring of the marvelous Byzantine civilization, the eastern empire was also threatened as the sixth century drew to a close. In the Balkans, Avars, Bulgars, and Slavs roamed the land. And in AD 570 a boy named Muhammad was born in the city of Mecca in the Arabian desert, whence would soon blow the storms of a militant new faith.

As the Christian church grew from a small, persecuted sect to the dominant religious force in the Mediterranean world, it absorbed the themes and symbols of diverse creeds and cults—ranging from Judaism, with its images of deliverance from oppression to the personal cult of the Roman emperor, with its emblems of unalloyed power. The Christian art that emerged from this process was a remarkably versatile instrument, capable of appealing to princes and ascetics, rebels and reactionaries.

Although images proved vital to the spread of Christianity, their very presence in places of worship posed a problem for the faithful. Like Jews, Christians were bound by the divine injunction against idol worship handed down to Moses: "You shall not make yourself a carved image or any likeness of anything in heaven or on earth beneath or in the waters under the earth; you shall not bow down to them or serve them." Some Christian authorities took this to apply even to scenes drawn from the scriptures; a council convening in Spain around AD 300 banned all pictures in churches, so as to preserve "what is reverenced and adored" from the taint of idolatry. But elsewhere, both Christians and Jews took a broader view, accepting pious images in their sanctuaries. In the Syrian town of Dura-Europus, a Christian church of the third century was decorated with a view of David fighting Goliath—an inspiring image for a struggling young faith— while a wall painting in a nearby synagogue showed David being anointed by Samuel as the future king of Israel.

Along with such Jewish heroes as David and Moses, who were seen by Christians as prefiguring Jesus, certain pagan deities were reinterpreted. Christian missionaries were reaching out to convert those who worshiped the powers inherent in nature, and artists did their part by adopting the colorful images of contemporary cults. Like the sun gods Mithras and Helios, Christ was shown rising radiantly into heaven; like the fabled musician Orpheus, who descended to Hades and returned, he was pictured with a lyre, taming wild animals with his song. Such icons might be frowned on by Church fathers, but they spoke to pagans with the force of revelation.

The growing appeal of Christianity was not long overlooked by Roman rulers. As Constantine and his successors turned from persecuting Christ's followers to seeking their blessing, Christian art took on an imperial tone. Beginning in the fourth century, proud basilicas rose up to house worshipers who had once gathered secretly in private homes. And the appointments of the sanctuaries—from the vibrant mosaics on the walls to the gleaming sacramental vessels at the altar—told of a Church that had come to terms with wealth and power. Devout rulers such as the Byzantine emperor Justinian were pictured in saintly guise, while Christ was portrayed as a king on his throne. Even in this time of triumph, however, Christian art was far from monolithic. The image of Christ the shepherd persisted alongside that of Christ the heavenly emperor, as the Church pursued its complex mission among the humble and the mighty alike.

Christian artists often selected themes from the Old Testament that appeared to foreshadow the triumphs and tribulations of Christ and his followers. In the eyes of the faithful, the fall of Adam left humankind in a state of sin that could be redeemed only through Christ's sacrifice. As St. Paul put it in the Epistle to the Romans: "One man's fall brought condemnation on everyone, so the good act of one man brings everyone life." St. Luke reinforced that connection in his gospel by tracing Christ's ancestry back more than seventy generations through David—the king chosen by God—to "Adam, son of God."

This allegorical approach to the Old Testament meant that even the simplest of biblical scenes could be layered with meanings for the devout. A favorite depiction in the catacombs where the Christians buried their dead was Moses raising his staff *(near right)* to draw water from the rock for the exiles in the desert. Christians facing persecution could view that picture as they honored their martyrs and rest assured that the God of Moses would comfort his people in their hour of need. But beyond that straightforward reading lay even richer symbolic ones. For the scene evoked Christ's role as the Redeemer, who said to the faithful that "he who believes in me will never thirst" and whose wound on the cross yielded not only blood but water, an emblem of renewal through baptism. And Moses' deed inspired thoughts as well of St. Peter, the Rock of the Church, who while awaiting execution in Rome brought forth a fountain in his cell, it was said, and baptized his jailers. Thus a single image loosed a stream of inspirational thoughts that affirmed the miraculous power of God's grace to triumph anew over oppression, want, and even death itself.

The prophet Samuel anoints David, a young shepherd from Bethlehem, as the future king of the Jews in this wall painting from the synagogue at Dura-Europus. According to scripture, God inspired Samuel to choose the youth over his older brothers *(background)* and later promised David that "your House and your sovereignty will always stand secure before me and your throne be established forever." The idea that a messiah descended from David would deliver the children of Israel from their woes remained current among Jews long after Jesus was proclaimed by his followers as the fulfillment of that dream.

In this scene from a Roman catacomb, the hand of Abraham is stilled by a voice from heaven before he can carry out the sacrifice of his son Isaac as commanded; the scapegoat that will take the boy's place stands beside the altar. The Old Testament theme of the father whose profound devotion leads him to offer up his son was central to Christian doctrine, as expressed in the Gospel of St. John: "For God so loved the world that he gave his only begotten Son."

Eve and Adam sit disconsolate, wearing pelts given them by God after they tasted of the forbidden fruit and grew ashamed of their nakedness.

Shadrach, Meshach, and Abednego sing praises to the Lord as the flames to which they have been consigned for refusing to worship the golden statue of Babylon lick harmlessly at their feet. Painted in a catacomb, this image of devout Jews being delivered by God spoke eloquently to Christians who themselves faced death for refusing to make offerings to the statue of the emperor. The three figures are garbed according to the Book of Daniel, which notes that they were thrown into the fiery furnace "fully clothed, cloak, hose, and headgear."

A figurine credited to a third-century Asia Minor sculptor shows Jonah being cast up by the sea monster to preach God's word. Jonah's ordeal was likened by Christ to his own impending burial and resurrection: "For as Jonah was in the belly of the sea monster . . . so will the Son of Man be in the heart of the earth."

Christianity was by no means the only popular creed to arise in the east and spread westward across the Roman Empire. Among its chief rivals in the second and third centuries was the cult of Mithras, a god first worshipped by Aryan tribes, who ranged from India to Mesopotamia. The devotees of Mithras believed that the forces of good and evil—embodied, respectively, by light and darkness—were ever at war. As the champion of good, Mithras came to be associated with the Greek sun god Helios and was often portrayed with a solar nimbus, or halo *(inset)*. Mithras's greatest feat had been to fight and kill a sacred bull, whose blood fertilized the earth. The image of Mithras slitting the bull's throat stood in the apse of the cult's shrines, which were built to resemble the dark cave in which the god accomplished the sacrifice.

Mithras's heroic deed fired the imaginations of soldiers throughout the Roman Empire, and the cult took on the character of a fraternal society, with initiation rites, loyalty oaths, and strict codes of conduct. This masculine bent put Mithraism at a disadvantage in relation to Christianity, which profited by the avid support of women: Of the first twelve recorded martyrs to the faith in the city of Carthage, five were women. Mithraism was handicapped as well by the fact that its central myth—the killing of the bull—bore all the marks of a rural fertility rite. The sacrifice of Christ, which replenished not the soil but human souls, proved more alluring in the urban centers that dominated Mediterranean culture. In time, Mithraism gave way, ceding to Christianity the symbol of the halo and a date for the celebration of Christ's birth—December 25, which the Mithraists had honored as the turning point in the sun's battle against night.

Other pagan traditions enriched the imagery of Christianity—among them the cult of Orpheus and the pastoral ideal of the shepherd, a type praised in pictures and verse long before Christ. Together, these sources helped fill out the mosaic of Christian art, adding a natural exuberance to the moral dimensions of the scriptures.

The nimbus—a radiant aura around the head of a deity or divine ruler—was an ancient symbol, in use as early as the third millennium BC. In representations of Mithras, this aura might take the form of a sunburst *(top)* or a pure circle of light. This early Christian image of Jesus inspired by the Greek cult of Helios combined the two attributes, showing solar rays emanating from a gleaming disk *(above)*. In time, Christian artists evolved a distinctive nimbus for their Lord—a halo inscribed with the cross.

Accompanied by his dog, Mithras slays the bull in this second-

century Roman relief. The scorpion stinging the bull and the snake lapping its blood were sent by the forces of evil to try to retrieve the bull's power before it nurtured the earth.

The fabled Greek hero Orpheus, who defied death and charmed the wild beasts with his music, was honored by some Christians as one who prefigured their Lord in the ability to triumph over nature. The Christian Orpheus below, carved in Greece in the fourth century, sits with lyre in hand, attended by a circle of real and imagined beasts. Among the creatures being pacified at right, in a fifth-century mosaic from a Jerusalem church, are two hybrids—a centaur and a satyr—reminders of the human savagery that Christ set out to quell.

The powerful Christian motif of the good shepherd carrying the stray back to his flock—as in the Roman statuette at left and the catacomb painting below—was closely related to the image of Christ as Orpheus with his soothing lyre. Both traditions were anticipated not only by pagan myths but by the biblical account of David, who while still a young shepherd played the harp for the tormented King Saul. David was said to have composed the Twenty-third Psalm, whose vision of God as an ever-watchful shepherd inspired Christ's parable of the lost sheep redeemed.

After Christianity won acceptance under Constantine, many Roman artists turned from secular to sacred themes. A sculptor who had begun his career portraying imperial campaigns on triumphal arches might end it carving biblical scenes on the sarcophagi of Christian converts. The sarcophagus shown here was crafted for one Junius Bassus, a prefect in Rome who was baptized on his deathbed in AD 359. The sculptor, true to his heritage, lent a classical look to the biblical motifs, framing each set of characters within columns and even including classical emblems such as the sky deity Caelus shown at right. But unlike earlier Roman reliefs of historical events, no sequence was imposed here; motifs from the Old and New Testaments were interspersed, as befits the wonders of a God who transcended history.

Some Roman aristocrats resisted the Christian tide and commissioned works that glorified the emperor—including one carving that portrayed him ascending to immortality. But the old imperial cult was doomed; henceforth, Roman rulers who aspired to heaven would first have to recognize Christ as king.

In the top central panel of the Bassus sarcophagus— shown in full above and in detail at right—Christ sits enthroned while Caelus, personifying the sky, supports him. The other upper frames show Abraham with Isaac (far left), the arrest of Peter, and Christ between two soldiers, facing Pilate.

This ivory panel carved around AD 400 shows a Roman emperor—perhaps Julian the Apostate, who staunchly opposed Christianity—rising to heaven as a god. In the lower half of the panel, a statue of the deceased emperor rides in a temple-shaped chariot drawn by four elephants. A funeral pyre looms in the background, crowned by a team of horses driven by a godlike youth and flanked by two soaring eagles, symbols of imperial power. At top, two winged genii, spirits assigned to watch over the emperor from birth to death, lift him up to join his divine predecessors; the signs of the Zodiac form an arc to the right, beside the radiant profile of Helios. The monogram at top is that of the wealthy Symmachus family, which sought to preserve pagan traditions.

Fashioned in Italy about the same time as the panel at left, this ivory carving portrays the Christian equivalent of the emperor's apotheosis—Christ being drawn up to heaven by the right hand of God as two apostles kneel in awe. At bottom, the resurrected Christ appears outside his sepulcher to three women, including Mary of Magdala. The tree at upper left may symbolize both the Tree of Knowledge in Eden, whose fruit brought about the Fall, and the Tree of Life there, which conferred immortality. Christian mystics identified Christ's cross with those trees, an association bolstered by the words Peter spoke to the high priest at Jerusalem after Christ's death: "It was you who had him executed by hanging on a tree. By his own right hand God has now raised him up to be leader and savior."

When Constantine shifted the capital of his empire from the banks of the Tiber to the mouth of the Bosporus in AD 330, he created an alluring new showcase for the Christian faith. Fourteen churches were erected in Constantinople within a century, and the task of decorating them drew artists from around the Mediterranean. The style they fostered was lavish and conspicuous, reflecting the tastes of the emperors themselves: Christian art had emerged from the shadows to flaunt its colors.

This elegant tone was not confined to Constantinople. Among the cities to echo it was the Italian port of Ravenna, on the Adriatic. Like Rome, Ravenna was overtaken by barbarians in the fifth century; but it maintained cultural ties with the east, and the mingling of Byzantine impulses and Italian artisanship yielded mosaics of kaleidoscopic brilliance. The tradition reached its peak after the emperor Justinian's troops drove the Goths from Ravenna in AD 540 and linked it officially to Byzantium. The mosaic at right, from Ravenna's San Vitale, shows a haloed Justinian presiding in spirit over the dedication of the church beside Maximian, archbishop of Ravenna. The emperor's own choice for the post, Maximian boasted all the trappings of an ecclesiastical viceroy—including a thronelike chair, crafted in Constantinople.

A similar sense of grandeur was expressed in other Christian cities united under Justinian. In the richest churches the chalices, plates, and missals were priceless works of art, reflecting an age-old impulse to pay tribute to one's lord. For centuries, pharaohs and caesars had been the recipients of such honors. Now the immutable metals, the flawless stones, were dedicated to a god-king whose appeal transcended that of his representatives on earth.

A gift from Justinian to Maximian, this ivory chair reflects the Byzantine skill at enlivening sacred art with worldly details. The front panels show John the Baptist (center) and the four evangelists, framed by a host of animals amid sinuous vines symbolizing the wine of the Eucharist.

Accorded a halo as God's
rightful regent, Justinian
holds a golden bowl in this
mosaic celebrating the
consecration of San Vitale
around AD 547; Maximian
clasps a jeweled cross. Al-

were seen as sanctified,
their dependence on God
was made clear by the
words spoken at their fu-
nerals: "Come, O emper-
or, thou art called by
the Emperor of emperors,

At once majestic and humble, the Virgin Mary sits like an empress on her throne, spinning wool by hand, as angels tell her of the savior she will bear. This mosaic was made in Rome to celebrate an edict extolling Mary as the Mother of God.

Christ resurrects Lazarus, who stands shrouded in a Roman-style sepulcher. Here as in other works of the day, the nimbus of Christ is marked by a cross to distinguish him from the plainly haloed saints and emperors.

*I*nset: Reclining like guests at a classical banquet, the apostles commune with Christ at the Last Supper. The artist has substituted loaves and fishes for the bread and wine cited in the scriptures—thus relating this first Eucharist to the miracle of Christ feeding the multitude.

Right: The three wise men carry gold, frankincense, and myrrh to honor the infant Jesus at Bethlehem. As befits magi from the east, they are dressed in the finest Byzantine fashion: spotted trousers of Persian design, richly brocaded tunics, and velvety cloaks clasped with jewels.

This silver gospel cover, crafted in the sixth century, lent an air of splendor to services performed at the Monastery of Holy Sion, on the coast of Asia Minor some 300 miles south of Constantinople. Set between two plants, the gilded cross evokes the biblical description of the Tree of Life, standing "in the middle of the garden," while the arch framing the scene represents the gateway to Paradise.

This fabulous gem-encrusted cross was a gift to the pope in Rome from Justin II, who succeeded Justinian as emperor in AD 565. Despite such grand gestures, relations remained strained between the Roman pontiffs—who claimed spiritual priority as heirs of St. Peter—and the Byzantine rulers, who often differed with Rome on questions of doctrine and had the power to enforce their views. During the seventh century, more than one pope would be summoned to Constantinople and chastised.

A chalice from Antioch portrays Christ as an inspired teacher with arms outstretched to his followers. The grapevine was long associated with the sacrificial cult of the wine god Dionysus; Christians embraced the pattern, mindful that Jesus had styled himself "the true vine" and had equated the wine of the Eucharist—held in vessels such as this—with his own blood.

Gilded patens such as this were used to carry the communion bread. The sixth-century artist modeled the first Eucharist after a contemporary communion service—presided over by two clerics. Christ appears twice at the center, serving parallel bands of six disciples each.

A fifth-century mosaic from the apse of Santa Pudenziana in Rome sums up the majestic prospects of an ascendant faith. Christ sits on his throne, flanked by the apostles. Soaring abov

DOMINVS ECCLESIAE
CONSER PVDENTI
VATOR ANAE

re symbols of the evangelists drawn from the Book of Revelation—man (Matthew), lion (Mark), ox (Luke), and eagle (John). At center, the cross rises like a jeweled scepter.

RENEWAL IN THE MIDDLE EAST

An empire hung in the balance as two armies closed for combat in the Iranian desert, maneuvering to the sounds of shouted commands, snorting horses, and the clink and rattle of armor and weapons. No detailed account of the clash that day in AD 224 would survive into the modern era, but the first troops into action on both sides probably were archers mounted on light ponies, who swooped toward the enemy at a gallop, then wheeled away while letting fly a savage hail of arrows. When one commander felt he had sufficiently softened up the opposition by this hit-and-run tactic, he ordered in his heavy cavalry. And his opponent, seeing the charge begin, no doubt issued the same command; both knew the shock value of momentum at this crucial moment. The cavalrymen, burdened by iron helmets and chain-mail suits that could weigh as much as eighty pounds, leveled their long lances and urged their big mounts into motion. The horses, too, were heavily draped in chain mail and lumbered along for some yards before gathering speed. But soon two great iron-clad masses of men and animals, bristling with lances, sun glinting from swords and ax blades, were thundering toward a mighty collision.

One of the forces was led by Artabanus V, ruler of the Parthian empire. It was his vast and once supremely powerful realm that was at stake. The other commander was Ardashir, an upstart from the small province of Persis in the Iranian heartland, who in recent years had by force and persuasion put together a coalition of vassal states to rise in revolt against their Parthian overlords. Ardashir's army had already beaten Artabanus's twice, but both times the Parthians had gotten away to fight again. This time the Persian would conclude the issue.

The forces crashed together with an impact that rent the desert air and tossed warriors from their mounts. Soon the field was a bloodied, thrashing tangle of horses and men, fighting and fallen. As the two sides hacked away at each other, it became increasingly clear that Ardashir had the victory. Then, somewhere in the melee, he apparently found and confronted his enemy Artabanus—at least that is the way Ardashir later had the event depicted in a rock carving commemorating his triumph. If the carving was accurate, Ardashir charged at a gallop and struck Artabanus with his lance, toppling the Parthian king and his horse. According to tradition, the antagonists continued their fight on foot until Ardashir clubbed Artabanus to death. To make sure the public would be in no doubt about the outcome, the Persian had Artabanus flayed, then displayed the king's skin in a temple.

This deadly violence marked the accession to imperial power of a dynamic new Persian dynasty. The Sassanids—they took their dynastic name from Ardashir's grandfather, Sassan—were to hold ironfisted dominion over a sprawling territory that one day would extend from the Persian Gulf to the Black Sea and from Syria's Mediterranean shore to Afghanistan. Supported by a state religion that imparted a divine aura

75

Three of the great Sassanian kings of Persia, each with a distinctive crown, appear on gold coins minted during their reigns. The bottom coin portrays Ardashir I (AD 224-241), founder of the ruling dynasty and victor over the Parthian Artabanus V in hand-to-hand combat. The middle coin shows Ardashir's successor, Shapur I (241-272), also a great warrior, who resoundingly defeated the legions of two Roman emperors. The coin at top portrays not only the sharp-featured Bahram II (276-293), but also his wife and a son who, as Bahram III, would rule for one year. It is the only Sassanid royal coin to show a monarch with his family.

to their authority, sustained by an army suited for warfare against both civilized enemies and barbarian hordes, Persia's rulers would direct their fervent energies toward restoring in all its glory a previous Persian empire, the one founded more than seven centuries earlier by Cyrus the Great.

In large measure, they succeeded. Yet their achievement came only at the cost of implacable hostility between them and their western neighbor, the Roman Empire, a hostility that after three centuries of warfare was to leave both antagonists drained and vulnerable to barbarian incursions from the north.

To the east, on the other hand, the Sassanids would dwell in a kind of symbiosis with India. In that land, too, a radiant new regime would arise during this era. For the Persians, the long and peaceful reign of India's Gupta dynasty would provide a much needed stability on the border shared by the two domains. At the same time, the powerful Sassanian frontier forces who fended off Hunnish assaults against their own lands also provided, more or less inadvertently, protection for the Guptas from barbarians who might otherwise make their way through mountain passes onto the Indian subcontinent. As long as that protective barrier held, India's astonishing culture could flourish in tranquility. Thus, Sassanian Iran and Gupta India would each in its own way shape a destiny made possible by circumstances arising from the victory of Ardashir in the bloodied desert sands.

Ardashir's father, Papak, had been king of Persis and a member of a priestly family. He presided over a threadbare court in the town of Istakhr and fulfilled his religious duties at the temple of Anahita. That goddess, who was associated with water and fire, was worshipped by Iranians with the sun-god Mithra and the Wise Lord, Ahuramazda, in a form of Zoroastrianism that had long ago lost its monotheistic character. Not far from Istakhr lay the ruins of Pasargadae and Persepolis, old capitals of the magnificent Achaemenids, and the crumbled palaces of Cyrus the Great, Darius I, and Xerxes, from whose loins Sassanian panegyrists would later claim lineal descent for Ardashir.

For all its past glories, Persis had long since been reduced to an insignificant vassalage, and its ruler was a minor figure among the countless provincial kinglets who owed their tenuous allegiance to the Great King of the Parthian empire. That was a condition that Ardashir, upon succeeding to his father's humble throne in AD 208, proceeded to change forthwith.

All his life, Ardashir had witnessed the decay and disintegration of the Parthian empire that ruled his land. From their earliest days, the Parthian kings had been dangerously dependent on the strength and loyalty of feudal lords who operated out of fiefdoms often far removed from the seat of central authority and who provided the realm with the cavalry required to maintain even a loose hegemony. It was the nature of such a feudalistic society to nourish itself on military success and to splinter when the central authority was weakened by reverses. During the first century AD, the empire had lost all the land it once controlled in northwest India, as well as Afghanistan, which the Parthians called Bactria. These territories had fallen to the Kushans, a group of tribes from the Asian steppes. And the Romans, who in the past had had many occasions to regret their wars with the Parthians, had lately been achieving some significant victories over them. As recently as the year 198, Rome's Septimus Severus had forcibly stripped the Parthian empire of the northern part of its Mesopotamian territory.

It naturally followed that the feudal warlords, increasingly contemptuous of the Great King and his waning power, should turn surly and even rebellious, retreating with their retinues into fortified enclaves and leaving the central Parthian government to fend for itself. Indeed, such were conditions on Iran's northern plateau that Parthia's rulers were no longer able even to provide protection for the east-west trade that once had been a source of riches for the empire. Hapless caravans along the Asian silk route fell easy prey to gangs of vagabond bandits, and merchants trafficking between China and Rome much preferred the southern sea route, which led through India and the Persian Gulf.

Clearly, opportunity lay here for an ambitious young king who dreamed of reviving an ancient empire. In making his move, Ardashir meant to forge a regime that would be fully supported by the Iranian warlords. By appealing largely to the self-interest of the nobles, the Parthian central government had lost their loyalty when the tide of events turned against it. Now, Ardashir sought to enlist them in a loftier cause by invoking images of Persia's proud past. Negotiating whenever he could, fighting whenever he had to, he first secured the fealty of all the local princes in Persis. Next he seized the neighboring province of Kerman, then Isfahan, Susiana, and Mesene.

All this took time, and it is perhaps an indication of the indolence of the Parthian

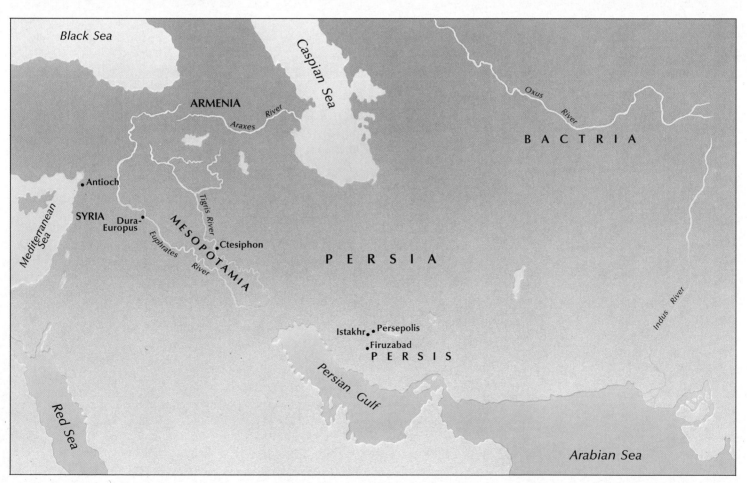

By AD 250 ambitious Sassanian kings had extended Persia's power across almost 2,000 miles, from the edges of the Roman world in Mesopotamia and Armenia through today's Iran to Bactria and the gateways of India in the mountainous Punjab and the Indus River valley.

regime that more than fifteen years passed before Great King Artabanus V finally bestirred himself sufficiently to accuse Ardashir of rebellion. By then, Ardashir had gathered too much strength to be put in his place by mere words. "God gave me this throne and this crown," he thundered, referring to the victories he had already won over provincial magnates. "I hope that I will be victorious over you, too," he warned Artabanus, "and take your head." It was this challenge, which no monarch who hoped to preserve his authority could ignore, that eventually drew Artabanus to his end in battle on a desert plain.

After his victory, Ardashir moved quickly to take over Parthia's western provinces in Mesopotamia. Within two years he controlled the Fertile Crescent and was calling himself the King of Kings, the title used by the Persian rulers of old. In an empire whose reason for being was based on pride in the Persian past, it was inevitable that Ardashir should seek the support of Persian institutions, especially the Zoroastrian religion, which the great Achaemenids had embraced.

Zoroastrianism was peculiarly unsuited for export. Many people unfamiliar with the faith, for instance, did not like the notion of exposing human corpses so that vultures or other carrion eaters could pick the bones clean — a practice intended to protect the sacred elements of earth, fire and water from corruption. But Zoroastrianism was a notably appropriate creed for Sassanian rulers. In its central thesis it envisioned a cosmic conflict in which the forces of righteousness, led by the wise god Ahuramazda with his army of angels, would eventually prevail over the powers of evil, under the wicked deity Ahriman and a host of demons and fiends.

As the earthly representative of the good god, Ardashir was surrounded by an aura of divinity that elevated him above other men. He wanted two forces—and only two forces—to command loyalty throughout his empire: the king who ruled by divine right and the god who granted it. As an inscription from the time of Ardashir's son would express the principle, "Church and state were born of one womb, joined together and never to be sundered."

In that amalgam, the King of Kings became the personal embodiment of *farr*—mystical majesty. To enhance his mystique, he made himself relatively inaccessible in a court that was characterized by solemnity and ceremony. Establishing the Persian *qurz*—an elaborate crown and an imposing mace or scepter—as emblems of royalty, he ordered that a holy fire be lighted in his name at the temple in Istakhr. Thereafter, events in the new Persian empire were dated from that moment, and Persians referred to this or that occurrence as having taken place, for example, "five years from the sacred flame of Ardashir."

As the official religion of the reborn state, Zoroastrianism of course had to have an apparatus, and Ardashir surrounded himself with Magi. These were members of the ancient priestly caste; they dressed themselves in long white robes and tall conical hats, and from their practices the word *magic* is derived. When a king died, the Magi would extinguish the holy fire and prepare a new one for his succaessor. As keepers of the sacred flame, they were in control of Sassanian coronations, calling upon astrologers and soothsayers to determine the most propitious moment for lighting the new fire—a process that on occasion delayed the crowning of a king for years after he had actually taken power.

The Magi not only attended Ardashir's court but followed the king into war, cleansing newly won territory of demons after a conquest. They dispensed the king's justice and presided over the empire's public administration, which included a corps

PERSIA'S MOUNTED WARRIORS

Made up of nobles—men who could afford horses—the Persian cavalry was among the best armed and armored fighting forces of its time. A cavalryman's chief weapon was an intimidating twelve-foot-long heavy spear called a *kontos*. He also carried a long iron sword and a short bow. For protection he wore a tunic and trousers of thick felt or leather and over that a long-sleeved coat of mail with overlapping metal scales. He also had a breastplate, a small shield, and an iron helmet with a hood of mail attached to protect the neck and cheeks.

of agents who spied on Persia's vassal lords, especially in the diverse and distant satellites along the borders.

Of the Magi in Ardashir's time, the most prominent was a priest named Tansar, who collected the scattered texts of Zoroastrianism and from them compiled the canonical *Avesta*, which became the central document of the faith, Persia's bible. It was the first step in creating a coherent church out of the local traditions that had been treasured by noble and priestly families, such as Ardashir's, and on which Zoroastrian doctrine had long been dependent.

Tansar became Ardashir's partner in the forging of the new empire, and when he spoke it was with the authority of the king. If trouble broke out, he was as likely as Ardashir to issue proclamations, and when one of Iran's lords got out of line, as they sometimes did, it was frequently Tansar who scolded him. "Know and understand," he wrote to an errant king named Gusnap, to emphasize the source of all authority, "that a crown is what he [Ardashir] sets upon your head and a realm is that which he entrusts to you."

While admonishing Gusnap, Tansar also found an opportunity to deliver a lecture about the social order of the empire. He described it as being divided into four estates. First came the clergy, including judges, temple guardians, and teachers as well as ascetics and priests. The second estate consisted of the foot soldiers and cavalry of Iran's military caste. Then came the third estate, of physicians, poets, and astronomers, along with accountants, historians, and judicial and administrative clerks. Finally there were the artisans, a category that included farmers and merchants. Above them all towered the king, with his arbitrary power even to punish the just and pardon the wicked if he so chose.

An obsession with order and a dread of weak government were the foundations of Ardashir's new state, and he missed no chance to build on them. Even in his architecture, he kept his majestic purpose clearly in mind, exploiting the possibilities for royal effect when he constructed his first palace in Persis atop the sheer face of a breathtaking gorge. To dramatize the daring of the location, he added a startling new architectural form called an iwan. This large dome was a shape that became classic in Iranian architecture during subsequent centuries. Fashioned from rough-hewn rock and gypsum plaster, the dome that crowned Ardashir's palace was an awesome symbol of power to the travelers who passed through the gorge beneath it.

Similarly, Ardashir's newly built city of Firuzabad was designed with the prestige of the empire in mind. Only two miles to the south of the palace, it was laid out in a circle, signifying that it was the focus of world power, and at each cardinal point of the compass a gate opened onto a trade route, leading to China, India, Rome, or Arabia. In fact, however, Firuzabad's role in commerce was largely a symbolic one. The real business was conducted at the empire's administrative capital of Ctesiphon. This city was actually a cluster of towns on both banks of the Tigris at a point where it flows close to the Euphrates and the two rivers are connected by canals,

King Shapur I of Persia *(below, right)* captures Emperor Valerian simply by grasping the sword-wielding Roman's left hand, as shown in a cameo made to Shapur's order shortly after the great Persian victory near Antioch in AD 260. It is doubtful that Shapur actually took Valerian prisoner in this fashion, but there is little question that the Roman Emperor and his legions were soundly defeated by the cavalry-led Persian force, so huge that a Roman witness wrote, "Everything so far as the eye could reach shone with glittering arms, and mail-clad cavalry filled hill and dale."

making the location a far more strategic entrepôt for world trade than Firuzabad.

At Ctesiphon, caravans coming from the west met those arriving from India and China. The western traders offered Babylonian carpets, precious stones from Syria, the Persian rouge that the Chinese used to color their eyebrows, and textiles from Syria and Egypt. In return for such items, the Chinese traded raw silk, which the Persians then exported, sometimes as finished cloth. Under the Sassanids, Persian textiles achieved the status of high art, and before long Iran had recovered its position as the great middleman in world commerce.

But—as was the case in virtually every land in that era—a flourishing trade was not nearly as important to the Iranian economy as agriculture. "There is no power without an army," wrote Ardashir, "no army without money, no money without agriculture, no agriculture without justice." Yet despite the premium placed on their endeavors by both the king and the *Avesta,* which assured farmers of many divine rewards, Iran's peasants must have felt that justice was in distinctly short supply. Prohibited from leaving their land in favor of other callings, subject to conscription as forced labor on government projects, Persia's tillers of the soil were also the victims of discriminatory head and land taxes. Urban inhabitants paid only the personal tax, although the profits of commerce and other remunerative vocations gave them much greater incomes than farmers had. Moreover, well-to-do city dwellers were apparently exempt from military drafts, while peasants by the thousands were dragooned into service as foot soldiers in the empire's huge armies.

At the head of those armies, the great barons still rode out from their fiefs to do battle. Yet Ardashir and his Sassanian successors took measures to ensure against the paralyzing disaffections that had afflicted the Parthian rulers. The real muscle of the army was provided by members of a lesser nobility who owed their status—and thus their loyalty—directly to the crown. At the same time, numerous royal relatives were appointed to keep an eye on things as provincial subkings. Ardashir, for example, assigned at least one of his sons and a number of brothers to govern districts of the realm, while his successor placed no fewer than four sons on petty thrones. As the system evolved, provincial service became a primary qualification for succession to the crown of the King of Kings.

With his military machine in good working order, Ardashir set out to resurrect the empire of the Achaemenids. He started by invading Roman Mesopotamia and Syria, and when Rome's Alexander Severus demanded that he cease and desist, Ardashir dispatched 400 soldiers, their weapons glittering with gold, to confront the emperor in Antioch and insist that the Romans abandon Asia altogether. Annoyed by such arrogant behavior, Alexander Severus promptly placed the entire Persian delegation under arrest. After some futile negotiations through diplomatic channels, there began a seesaw series of wars that would continue for three centuries, with neither of the great civilized antagonists able to achieve permanent mastery over the other—and with barbarians becoming the only beneficiaries as both the Persian and Roman empires were bled of their strength.

After Ardashir's death in AD 241, he was followed to the throne by his son Shapur I, an imperialist after his father's own heart. With little delay Shapur completed a job already begun by Ardashir—the subjugation of the Kushans in western Bactria and northwest India. Once the crown had been placed on his head, Shapur expanded on Ardashir's royal title by styling himself *Shahansha i Eran u Aneran,* "King of Kings of

Iran and Non-Iran," and to prove his point he immediately resumed the struggle with Rome. He was defeated by the troops of the emperor Gordian—one of a welter of Roman rulers and would-be rulers who contended for power in a long period of imperial turmoil that followed the death of Alexander Severus. But after Gordian's death, Shapur forced the next Roman emperor, a Transjordanian who was known as Philip the Arab, to give up Armenia to Persia. Armenia controlled the southern exits from the passes of the Caucasus Mountains, through which barbarians from Russia could invade southwest Asia, and it was therefore crucial to the defenses of both empires. (This was not the last time the Persians and Romans would clash over Armenia.) With Shapur's next thrust, around AD 256, he swept through Syria to the gates of the great commercial city of Antioch, where yet another Roman emperor Valerian—the fourth on the throne since Philip the Arab—had established headquarters. Despite heavy losses, Valerian checked the Persian advance, but four years later Shapur was back. This time he not only crushed Valerian's army but took the emperor prisoner, treacherously seizing him during a conference arranged to discuss a truce. Shapur returned to Iran loaded with loot and with enough Roman captives, including engineers, to build an immense dam at Shoshtar, in eastern Babylonia, for irrigation purposes. Valerian apparently spent the rest of his life as a prisoner, by some accounts in a palace where he dwelt in luxurious style. At home, Shapur's affairs were complicated by a priest named Kartir, who had succeeded old Tansar as head of the Magi. Despite Ardashir's sponsorship of Zoroastrianism as the religion of the state, both he and Tansar had been generally tolerant of Iran's substantial Jewish population and a growing number of Christians. Not so Kartir: A Zoroastrian zealot, he organized the Magi around a rigid orthodoxy and planned to persecute as heretics all those of other faiths whom he failed to convert.

In the early days of his reign, Shapur went along with Kartir's oppressive notions, but the increasing power of the Magi soon appeared as a much greater threat than the religious minorities could conceivably be. Shapur thereupon reversed his policy, forbade the Magi to continue their persecution, and declared that "all men of whatever religion should be left undisturbed and at peace in their belief in the several provinces of Persia."

Remarkably, Shapur's edict extended even to the followers of a creed that tended to undermine the exalted status of the Sassanian rulers as earthly agents of the universal forces of righteousness. As promulgated by a self-proclaimed prophet named Mani, this heresy held that all religions had been corrupted by time and that the divine message was always the same, whether delivered by Zoroaster, Buddha, Abraham, Noah, or Jesus Christ. More to the point, Manicheanism was Zoroastrianism turned inside out: It argued that the armies of the good, despite the help they were presumably getting from the Sassanian kings, were losing out to the legions of evil and that redemption could come only when common people and monarchs accepted a harsh and celibate life that was the very antithesis of Sassanian sumptuousness.

Nonetheless, Shapur accepted Mani himself at the imperial court and permitted missionaries to spread his message throughout the empire. Soon Manicheanism posed a serious threat to Kartir's orthodox priesthood. All this came to an end, however, after the death of Shapur in AD 272, when Kartir regained his influence at court and saw to it that Mani was arrested. The prophet died after spending less than a month in prison. His authority secure, Kartir remained chief of the Magi throughout the reign of four more Persian kings, dominating religious affairs and building the

Magnificently crafted in gold and silver, objects such as these served as emblems of Sassanian monarchs' power and wealth. The great bust probably is an idealized portrait of the long-lived King Shapur II. Only slightly smaller than life-size, it was hammered from a single piece of silver. The plate, made about AD 500, lauds the hunting prowess of a later Persian monarch; the figures of the king, his horse, and the fleeing rams were made separately, then soldered to the silver plate and gilded. The rams' horns and the king's bow were accented by a shiny black sulphur compound.

power of the Zoroastrian clergy to rival and eventually to surpass that of the nobility.

By the time Shapur II came to power in AD 309, the state and the church had become virtually indistinguishable in the Persian establishment. As fanatical a Zoroastrian as any of his priests, Shapur II found it only natural to double the taxes of Christians to support his endless wars. When they protested, he embarked on a merciless forty-year persecution of Christians, Jews, and other religious minorities.

Indeed, during his seventy-year reign—by far the longest of any Sassanian king— Shapur II would prove a ruthless adversary to any who opposed him. Waging war against the inhabitants of the parched Arabian desert, he forced their submission by filling their wells with sand. After putting down a revolt at Susa, he turned his elephants to pulverizing the ruins of the city beneath their giant feet. Upon capturing an Armenian king, he ordered the man blinded.

He was perhaps the most relentless of the Sassanids in conducting his family's long-running feud with the Roman Empire (or, by now, the Eastern Roman Empire, ruled from Constantinople). Repeatedly marching onto the war-torn plains of Mesopotamia, he placed the Roman fortress city of Nisibis under siege at least three times in a period of twelve years without ever managing to break into the stronghold. Undiscouraged, he returned to Mesopotamia in 359, soundly defeated a Roman army under the emperor Constantius, and in 363 seized the citadel of Singara. A few years later, apparently determined to end the Sassanian menace once and for all, the Roman emperor Julian, in conjunction with a force of Armenians, pushed across the Tigris and neared Shapur's capital at Ctesiphon. Before he could attack the city, however, he was killed in a fierce battle fought near Samarra, and his army soon found itself threatened rather than threatening.

His successor, Jovian, was proclaimed emperor by the legions in Mesopotamia. In order to save his men from their desperate plight, Jovian was obliged to surrender to Persia all Roman lands east of the Tigris. He also conceded that Armenia, control of which the Romans had begun contesting again late in the third century, was outside the Roman sphere of influence. Tireless though he was in his wars against the Romans, Shapur must have welcomed the respite that was offered by his treaty with Jovian. For by this time the Persian king must have been deeply concerned about the security of his eastern frontier, where, as early as 350, a fearsome new enemy had appeared: the White Hun.

In later ages, the origins and racial character of the White Huns, also called Hephthalites or Ephthalites, would be clouded in mystery: No one would know for certain who they were or where they came from. They may have been a branch of the Xiongnu, the so-called barbarian people from Mongolia who in this same period seized control of northern China. If so, they were also probably ethnic cousins of the dreaded Huns who invaded Europe under the leadership of Attila, although there were noticeable racial dissimilarities between the two groups, as the name White Huns indicated. "The Ephthalites are of the Hunnish race and bear the Hunnish name," reported a sixth-century Byzantine writer, Procopius, "but they are completely different from the Huns we know. They alone among the Hunnish peoples have white skins and regular features with big eyes." Attila's Huns, on the other hand, were generally Mongoloid in appearance. Nonetheless, both groups could have stemmed from the Xiongnu, whose numbers may have included more than one race. Early Chinese annals described at least some of the Xiongnu as having "red hair, green eyes, and white faces."

Procopius also noted distinct cultural differences. The White Huns, he said, "are not a wandering people and do not move from one place to another like the general Huns, but live under a king and have a constitution of their own to guide administration. Their behavior toward their neighbors and colleagues is severe and frank and resembles very much the Romans in this respect."

Although his description may have applied to Hephthalites in his own time (the sixth century) it probably was not so accurate a picture of those encountered by Shapur II two centuries earlier. When the White Huns first appeared on the northeastern margins of the Sassanian empire, they still were nomads who lived on horseback, depended on cattle and hunting for their livelihood, and frequently moved from place to place in search of fresh pastures or more game. Their culture most likely closely resembled that of earlier Xiongnu people described by the Chinese. They bedded down in dome-shaped tents of felt stretched over lattice frames and probably dressed in felt or skin trousers strapped tight at the ankles, leather boots, leather or fur upper garments, and fur caps. The men may have shaved their heads, leaving a tuft of hair on top and two short braided pigtails behind their ears, and many of them wore long, dangling wooden earrings.

Unique among Hunnish peoples—and rare for any society—the White Huns practiced polyandry, although how many husbands a woman had is not clear. Powerful wizards, shamans, and witch doctors guided their worship of the sun, moon, ancestors, and several supernatural beings. Their solemn rites, such as drinking the blood of a sacrificed white horse to seal a covenant, were sometimes viewed as repugnant by more settled peoples. And some of their behavior was, as Procopius said, severe. To enforce their simple laws, they crushed the ankles of minor offenders and executed those guilty of major crimes. To mourn the deaths of husbands, White Hun widows slashed their cheeks so that blood flowed with their tears. Boys were trained to fight on horseback from an early age and were made warriors as soon as they could pull a full-sized bow. Enemies developed a special fear of White Hun arrows, which were barbed so they would badly tear the flesh if pulled from wounds. To the White Huns, all was fair in war. They felt no dishonor in retreating when outnumbered.

Shapur II repulsed the White Huns' initial attempts to invade his realm; but they settled in the northeastern fringe areas, which had formerly been occupied by the Kushans, and continued their clamorous efforts to break through the Persian frontier. To Shapur's beleaguered successors they were a bane for more than a century. Then,

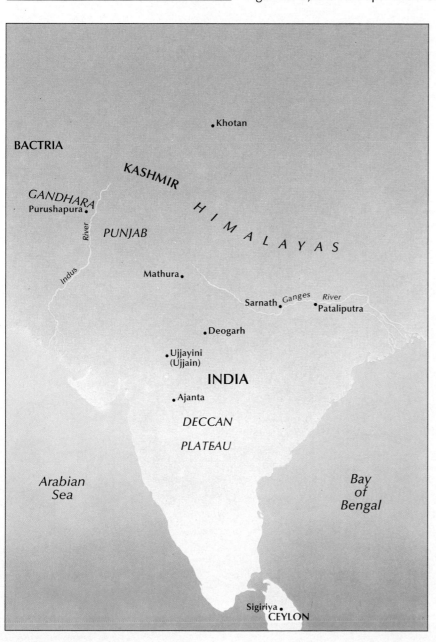

To the southeast of Persian territory India's Gupta emperors, initially rulers of a small kingdom straddling the Ganges around Sarnath, expanded their benevolent, prosperous rule until they controlled territories stretching across northern India from the Bay of Bengal all the way to the Arabian Sea.

The art of the Gupta empire captures a court life of leisure and refinement. As shown in a mural *(above)* from the Ajanta caves in Hyderabad, courtiers lived in handsome palaces with armies of servants. To while away the hours there was wine and betel nut, a mild narcotic. Emperors and their retinues had ample time for the arts. According to the *Kama Sutra,* sixty-four artistic skills were required of the families of princes. Singing was the most important, followed by the playing of such musical instruments as the gourd lute shown in the terra-cotta relief at right.

in 484, a Sassanian king by the name of Peroz led an Iranian army east to settle the Hephthalite problem. According to those who chronicled the era, including Procopius, the White Huns won by trickery. They dug a great pit or trench, lined with sharpened stakes by some accounts, and somehow contrived to have the Iranians fall into it. Peroz was killed, his army defeated, and the Sassanians ignominiously became tribute-paying vassals of the White Huns, who had established an empire of their own that stretched from northeastern Iran across Central Asia to Chinese Turkestan.

Once they had broken the protective Persian barrier, the White Huns poured into northwest India, killing and looting as they went. In Persia, the Sassanians would endure, survive, and eventually drive out the Hunnish intruders. In India, however, their arrival was the beginning of the end of one of the most glorious eras that land ever experienced, the rule of the Gupta dynasty.

Oddly enough, the sophisticated civilization of the Guptas, which was to be brought down by the barbarian White Huns, was built on foundations laid by other barbarians. These were a group of vaguely related Central Asian peoples who in about 50 BC had attacked and occupied Bactria, the land that much later would be called Afghanistan, settling in the harsh mountain country of the Hindu Kush. Around the middle of the first century AD, they united behind a single tribe, the Kushans, and came to be called by that name. And about that same time they began to look south and dream of better lands.

For the squabbling petty kingdoms of northern India, the Kushan threat was nothing new. Foreign invasion had long been a recurring feature of Indian life. During the second century BC, Greeks—ensconced in Bactria since the days of Alexander the Great—had taken advantage of India's disarray and had annexed a number of enclaves. Less than 100 years later, Scythian tribes, forced southward by the migratory wave that included the Kushans, shoved out the Greeks. After them came the Parthians, who in turn pushed the Scythians deeper into west central India, where they settled and became known as Shakas.

Each group had left its mark on India. In addition to promoting Western theories of astrology and medicine, the Bactrian Greeks probably influenced the development of Sanskrit drama by the example of their Greek theaters and plays. The Scythians had established a tidy trade connection with Central Asia, which would continue for long after they were dispossessed. And, according to legend, the Parthians brought with them the apostle Thomas, who introduced Christianity to India before dying in the south near Madras.

Yet only the Kushans managed to establish a stable and substantial empire, which would endure for some 200 years. And although their greatest ruler, Kanishka, was depicted on his coins wearing the kind of heavily padded clothing that had shielded his people from the shrieking winds of the steppe, his reign offered evidence of how barbarian peoples could absorb—and even improve on—the ways of the civilized lands they had conquered.

Kanishka came to power around AD 78 and ruled for twenty years from his capital at Purushapura (modern Peshawar, Pakistan) in Gandhara, a position that commanded the Khyber Pass leading through the mountains from Bactria and Iran to India. From there his armies extended his holdings—which already included the old Kushan lands in Bactria and Central Asia—through the Punjab to encompass most of northern India, from the Indus River valley in the west all the way to the Ganges Basin in the east. According to some accounts, Kanishka also reached out along the old silk trade route north of the Himalayas to Kashgar, Yarkland, and Khotan on the approaches to China, in the process borrowing for his own use the title of the Han dynasty's emperor—Son of Heaven.

Another major trade route between the Mediterranean and the Far East dropped down from Bactria through the Khyber Pass and across northern India to the Bay of Bengal, and Kushan centers along this corridor thrived. The river city of Mathura in the center of northern India, for example, became a rich export outlet for ivories and other luxury goods from India's west coast. But it was the province of Gandhara that lay at the heart of the Kushan commercial network. Merchant caravans of camels, oxen, and donkeys, laden with Chinese lacquers, Egyptian glassware, and Roman sculptures, traveled back and forth through Purushapura accompanied by monks, poets, artists, and musicians whose ideas found a ready reception at Kanishka's court.

Kanishka was celebrated as much for his cosmopolitan outlook as for his conquests, for his wisdom as well as his wealth. He was exposed to the creeds of the Hellenes, Christians, and Zoroastrians who mixed freely in his capital, along with the stronger influences of the Brahmans, keepers of India's ancient Hindu faith, and the Buddhists, who followed the teachings of the fifth-century BC religious philosopher Siddartha Gautama, known as the Buddha—the Enlightened. Indeed, if Kanishka was not himself a formal convert to Buddhism, he was certainly one of the religion's great patrons. His enthusiastic support found long-lasting expression in a fourteen-story wooden tower he erected outside Purushapura as a monument to the Buddha. Located near a monastery that Kanishka endowed as a wellspring of Buddhist learning, the tower would still be standing some 600 years later, transfixing passing Chinese pilgrims with its grace.

Kushan artists and sculptors were the first to depict the Buddha as a human figure instead of an abstact symbol. In token of the cosmopolitan outlook that had come to pervade the barbarians from the steppes, Kanishka's Buddha appeared in the flowing robes of a hellenized Roman.

Far more significant than his earthly edifices and images was Kanishka's interest in Buddhist thought. He gathered around himself renowned Buddhist scholars such as Nagarjuna, who was to help found a new branch of Buddhism, and the poet-dramatist Asvagosha, who wrote in Sanskrit, the ancient, long-neglected language of the learned Brahman priests. Asvagosha composed one of the earliest of the classical Sanskrit poems, *Buddha Charita,* or *The Life of Buddha,* and Kanishka himself may have tried his hand at a long Sanskrit poem.

At least partly because of contacts with Christianity and its promise of human redemption, a transformation in Buddhist theology—begun long before Kanishka came to power—found official sanction during his reign. A cult of the future Buddha, Maitreya, had spread among the religion's sects during the first century AD. Rejecting the notion of Buddha as a great teacher who had turned his back on humanity to find tranquility in Nirvana, many Buddhists now held that Buddha, far from having been a mere mortal, was the manifestation on earth of a divine spirit, through whose agency human salvation might be achieved.

Under Kanishka's sponsorship, the revisionists held a council in Kashmir. There, during six months of discussion, they developed the doctrinal authority for Mahayana (Great Vehicle) Buddhism, which, with its pantheon of saints, called bodhisattva, and its elaborate metaphysical trappings, celebrated Buddha as the godly savior of humanity. The Buddhist brotherhood in Ceylon boycotted the Kashmir council and promoted its own, more traditional Buddhism, which became known as Hinayana, or "Lesser Vehicle." But it was the visionary Mahayanism that would eventually spread most widely in China, where it replaced Confucianism as the prevailing faith.

About AD 100, the rule of the enlightened Kanishka came to a sorry end when, according to legend, he was smothered by some treasonous lieutenants. After his death, the Kushans continued in control of northwest India for more than a century before the Sassanian Persians under Shapur I toppled them. But the Persians were too busy trying to maintain their gains in the west against the ambitions of the Romans to linger long in India. In effect, their defeat of the Kushans left a power vacuum there, and in the dawn of the fourth century a new dynasty arose to fill it.

Although the origins of the Guptas are disputed, it seems likely that the founder of the dynasty stemmed from an obscure line of local rulers, probably in Bihar. Although there is no evidence that he was of Mauryan descent, he bore the name of the first great Mauryan king—Chandra Gupta. As an ambitious young man who aspired to the eminence of his namesake, he was shrewd enough to marry a princess of the Licchavi clan, rulers of a powerful state in the eastern Ganges region. Presumably using his Licchavi connections, Chandra Gupta gained control of that vital artery of Indian commerce, the Ganges, and by the time of his death in 335 he had extended his sway over a sizable piece of northeastern India.

On his deathbed, he urged his son to "rule the world," and, at least within South Asia, Samudra Gupta did his best to comply. Calling himself the "Exterminator of Kings," he overthrew nine of them in northern India and brought Kashmir within his domain. He also expanded the Gupta frontiers westward to the Punjab, forced at least a dozen kings as far south as the Deccan to pay him homage, and even reduced the king of Ceylon to vassalage. In celebrating his conquests, he revived the ancient Great Horse Sacrifice, a sacred Vedic rite in which a white stallion consecrated for the purpose was sacrificed and chopped apart by ax-wielding priests. The ritual was reserved for conquerors.

Still, it was in the reign of Samudra's son, Chandra Gupta II, that the Gupta dynasty reached the zenith of its imperial power, spreading completely across North India from Bengal to the Arabian Sea. And it was after he had by force of arms become the paramount sovereign of North India that he demonstrated his true greatness by becoming an apostle

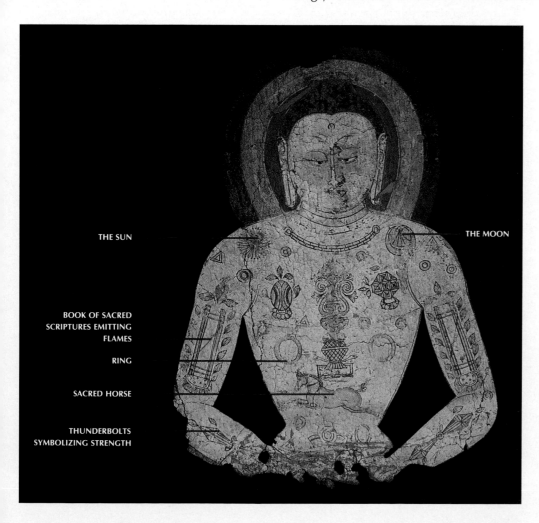

THE SUN

THE MOON

BOOK OF SACRED SCRIPTURES EMITTING FLAMES

RING

SACRED HORSE

THUNDERBOLTS SYMBOLIZING STRENGTH

By Gupta times the Buddha had evolved into an all-powerful deity whose attributes included many drawn from Hindu concepts, as shown in the sixth-century painting at left, an image of the *Vairochana*—or "cosmic"—Buddha, the creator. The emblem in the Buddha's chest, for example, was associated with the Hindu creation god, Vishnu, and his wife, Lakshmi. Below it are the Hindu signs for the ocean and the mountains. The world came from the ocean, in Hindu lore, along with the sun, moon, and other natural forces, represented by symbols on the Buddha's arms and torso.

A pair of naked and emaciated ascetics, their thin legs drawn up, meditate on the Buddha's teachings in a Gupta period terra-cotta tile. Such ascetics, who renounced all possessions to seek spiritual salvation, were deeply respected in ancient India. The tile, from a Buddhist temple at Harwan in central Kashmir, also shows some vividly modeled geese *(bottom)*—symbols of paradise frequently used as decoration in Buddhist art.

of peace and a devoted patron of the arts. During the remaining years of his life, Chandra Gupta II brought his far-flung realm to the crest of its cultural splendor and inspired among its peoples a new sense of personal freedom, religious tolerance, and social order.

As Chandra Gupta's reign neared its end, for example, a Chinese Buddhist monk named Faxian could wander from one end of the empire to the other, noting that "the inhabitants are rich and prosperous and vie with each other in the practice of benevolence." In the emperor's capital at Pataliputra, he found that hospitals were open free of charge to "the poor of all countries, the destitute, crippled, and diseased." And as he made his pilgrimage to Buddhist shrines, Faxian had no fear of being molested, or even questioned, despite the fact that he was a stranger, a foreigner, and a devoted Buddhist scholar in an India that by now had become dominated by Hinduism.

Under the Kushans, the close relationship between the Buddhist priesthood and the ruling classes had diluted the popularity of the religion among India's masses. Moreover, while the Buddhist hierarchy enjoyed the affluence and the influence that had come its way thanks to royal sponsorship, and while Buddhist theologians argued endlessly over abstruse metaphysical points, the Brahmans, who comprised the priestly caste of the Hindus, had gone into the Indian countryside, teaching, learning, and proselytizing. Although the Guptas tolerated Buddhism and other creeds, they strongly supported Hinduism. In their benign society the religion expanded to include many different devotional cults, such as those of Vishnu, protector and preserver of the world and moral order, and Shiva, among whose several manifestations was that of a destroyer wearing a wreath of skulls. For the most part, the Brahmans seemed content to let the cults develop without interference, confident in their belief that all such worship led to the same goal and that the ultimate godhead lay beyond any divisions fostered by the sects.

At the same time, however, the Brahmans tightened their hold on Gupta society by codifying their religious teachings in the *Dharma Shastras,* which comprehensively catalogued behavior in every conceivable circumstance for members of each of the Hindu castes—hereditary divisions of society that ranked all Indians from the priestly Brahmans on top down to the despised untouchables at the bottom. For example, the *Dharma Shastras* declared that on meeting, young men of the same caste should embrace, but a young man encountering an elder of his own caste or anyone of a higher caste should bow or even touch his superior's foot.

The resurgence of Hinduism sparked Indian creativity. Both science and literature took on new life. In the universities that sprouted across the Gupta domains, Indian astronomers—among the most famous, two named Varahamihira and Aryabhata—were far in advance of their counterparts in the rest of the world. Aryabhata, for one, knew that a round earth rotated on its axis and worked with sophisticated mathematical tools such as the value of pi, negative quantities, and quadratic equations. Indian mathematicians had discovered the concept of zero, and they employed decimal numbers with a place-value system of numerical notation. That is, a digit's value depended on its position; the number 2 meant 20 if located two places to the left of the decimal, or two-tenths if positioned one place to the decimal's right. This made calculation rapid and relatively easy. (Such decimal numbers would remain chiefly tools for experts until the Arabs of a later period popularized them, revolutionizing marketplace arithmetic.)

The Gupta period was an era of particularly impressive accomplishments in literature. The Brahmans not only preserved and wrote commentaries on the ancient sacred texts called the *Vedas,* they also contributed to secular Sanskrit classics. Both of India's two great epic poems, the *Mahabharata* and the *Ramayana,* found final written form now, after centuries of oral transmission and elaboration. The myths of the non-Vedic but equally ancient *Puranas* also made their way to the written page, as did fables and fairy tales of all kinds. Indian fables traveled well. A collection of stories called the *Panchatantra,* about animals who talked as if they were human, attracted readers in Baghdad, Byzantium, and Cairo as well as in northern Indian cities such as Pataliputra, and eventually reached Europe, where they were the source of many folktales and pieces of European literature.

The Sanskrit classics produced in Gupta India were by no means limited to transcriptions of traditional tales. A complex courtly style developed in Sanskrit verse, which like most court poetry tended to be highly ingenious but somewhat artificial, its rich and closely knit texture depending on wordplay, obscure meanings, and the special sensibilities of the cognoscenti. One poem, for example, had one meaning when read from left to right but could also be read from right to left to convey another, completely different, meaning. Intrigued by the cleverness of such verse, the Guptas often held tournaments and competitions, challenging poets to match their wit and talent on an assigned theme. The poets responded with energy and enthusiasm, composing riddles and ornate rhymes, using puns and double entendres—anything to win. And when all else failed, they were not above slipping the judges a bribe.

Sanskrit drama was designed especially for educated audiences, and few outside the noble and cultured classes could share in its appeal. Greek drama may well have influenced Indian stagecraft, but Gupta playwrights followed a set of rigid rules and

Heads shaved, dressed in ragged garments, mendicant Buddhist monks pray in a mural from the Ajanta caves. During the Gupta period, thousands of Buddhists, young and old, wandered the land to beg for food while they sought self-mastery and enlightenment by following their great teacher's rules. The monks were forbidden not only to lie, steal, and kill but also to drink alcohol, sleep in comfortable beds, wear ornaments, covet gold and silver, seek worldly entertainment, or eat anything after noon.

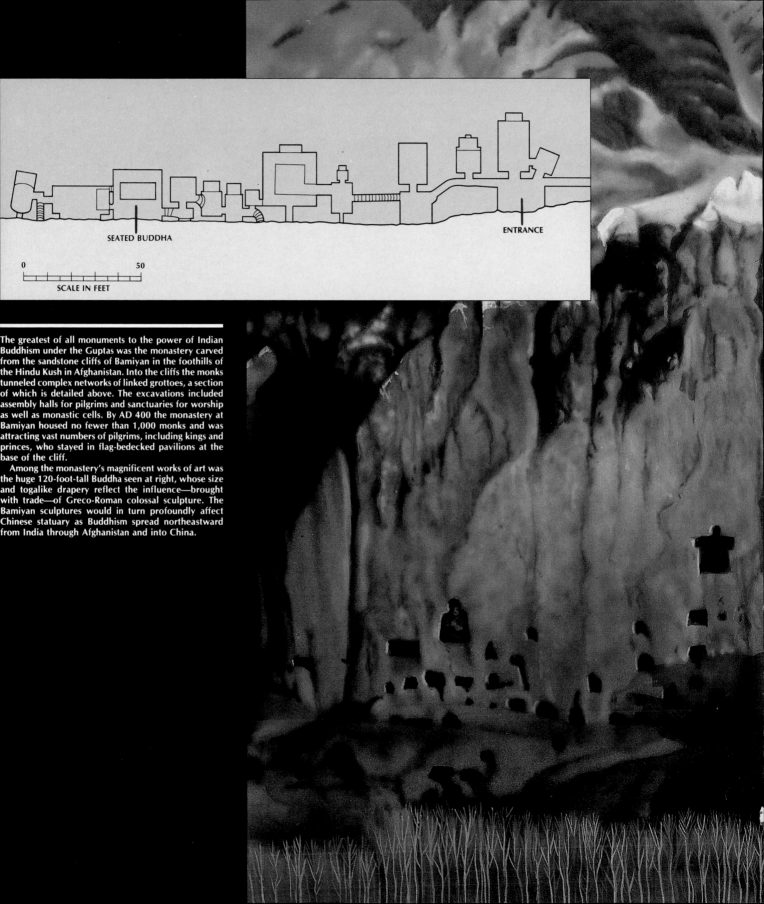

SEATED BUDDHA

ENTRANCE

0   50

SCALE IN FEET

The greatest of all monuments to the power of Indian Buddhism under the Guptas was the monastery carved from the sandstone cliffs of Bamiyan in the foothills of the Hindu Kush in Afghanistan. Into the cliffs the monks tunneled complex networks of linked grottoes, a section of which is detailed above. The excavations included assembly halls for pilgrims and sanctuaries for worship as well as monastic cells. By AD 400 the monastery at Bamiyan housed no fewer than 1,000 monks and was attracting vast numbers of pilgrims, including kings and princes, who stayed in flag-bedecked pavilions at the base of the cliff.

Among the monastery's magnificent works of art was the huge 120-foot-tall Buddha seen at right, whose size and togalike drapery reflect the influence—brought with trade—of Greco-Roman colossal sculpture. The Bamiyan sculptures would in turn profoundly affect Chinese statuary as Buddhism spread northeastward from India through Afghanistan and into China.

dramatic principles that were very much their own. Their work was aimed at creating a dispassionate delight in the contemplation of life as a whole. Tragedy was entirely alien to their culture, and audiences were supposed to leave the performance of a Sanskrit play feeling serene and peaceful.

Chandra Gupta II composed in Sanskrit himself, and it was said that his auxiliary court at Ujjain was graced by the "Nine Jewels" of Indian literature. Foremost among these outstanding writers was Kalidasa, whose name means "Slave of Kali." (Kali was the Hindu goddess of, among other things, poets.) Kalidasa would come to occupy a position in Indian literature as exalted as that of Shakespeare in the English language. As the land's most celebrated poet and playwright, he displayed a love of both undisciplined nature and the pomp of court ceremony. Of his seven works, *Shakuntala* was his masterpiece. Based on a tale from the *Mahabharata,* the play took its title from the achingly beautiful young heroine who captured the heart of a king. The complicated plot—in which the two lovers marry, are forced to separate, and finally reunite—belied the sensuality, inventiveness, and eloquence that gave the play its classic elegance.

One of the best known works of the era was an erotic compendium called the *Kama Sutra,* or *The Science of Love.* The book would later become famous in the West as a risqué classic. But it and other treatises on the same subject were not only respectable but integral to genteel Indian society, since expertise in *kama,* or love, was one of four goals to which right-minded people aspired. (The other three were *dharma,* or moral law or duty; *artha,* or the proper use of money; and *moksha,* or spiritual liberation.) In its depiction of the cultured, leisured life of Gupta citizens, the *Kama Sutra* embodied the opulent ideals of the times.

Buddhist art also reached its apogee in the Gupta period. Sculptures of the Buddha chiseled at Sarnath in northeastern India and Mathura in the north central region seemed serene and simple enough to warm the heart of any Hellene. At the central India Buddhist site of Ajanta, artists painted frescoes on dim walls and dark ceilings that reflected the refined fashions of the Gupta court, with its lavish hairstyles, abundant jewelry, and rich costumes. And on Buddhist memorials called stupas, magnificently detailed carvings depicted cities besieged, military processions, faithful worshippers, elephants plodding through the jungle, lions, peacocks, mythic creatures, and a riot of floral designs.

Hindu artists, meanwhile, were creating more humanistic depictions of their own deities and were becoming particularly adept at creating sensual images of women. In the architecture of their religious edifices, the Gupta Hindus were innovators who set a style from which later temples would develop. Each of the temples was dedicated to a single deity—Vishnu, Shiva, or one of the many forms of the mother goddess—and at each shrine the god's icon was placed in an inner sanctum strongly reminiscent of a cave.

In fact, Indians had always felt that caves were sacred, and for ages they had been improvising havens of worship inside natural caverns. Later, they began not only to enlarge some of the caves but to excavate rocky prominences and even mountainsides to create grottoes.

When the architects finally turned to erecting freestanding temples, they made the buildings resemble mountains on the

As Buddhism spread to China, Hinduism gained prominence in India under the Guptas. This monumental fifth-century sculpture portrays Hinduism's most revered deity, Vishnu. Seven of the 1,000 heads of Ananta, the cosmic serpent, loom over the god, while his wife, Lakshmi, massages his feet. According to Hindu belief, Vishnu created the world from the chaos of primeval ocean and provided the inner cohesion that kept the universe intact. At the top, five other deities pay homage while sitting on animals and plants symbolic of their divinity: Karttikeya on a peacock, Indra on an elephant, Brahma on the lotus, and Shiva and Parvati on a bull. Directly behind Lakshmi are a female attendant and the minor god Garuda, who in the form of an eagle transported Vishnu through the heavens.

outside and caves within, with small, darkened sanctuaries where no natural light could penetrate. Generally, the Hindu temple developed during the Gupta age was simple in form and modest in size. It sat on a raised platform within a paved rectangle. Topped by a flat roof and girdled by a porch displaying sculptured reliefs, the temple was entered through a square hall that led to the heart of the structure, where the deity's image was housed. (This was most commonly Brahma, the Hindu creator god, but some temples sheltered other prominent deities.) Such temples were designed in imitation of a sacred geometric diagram called a mandala—a square divided into smaller squares by a grid of crisscrossing lines, the whole representing the Hindu cosmos in miniature. Guardians of the sun and moon and other astronomical divinities occupied the outer squares of the concentric pattern. In the central square resided Brahma.

To build the temples, workers, often accompanied by their families, settled in a camp near the site for the year or so it took to complete the job. Government officials kept peace in the camps and imposed fines for delays in work or the delivery of materials. Doctors, barbers, cooks, and other functionaries lived in the camps and saw to the needs of the workers. Menials toted drinking water and refreshments as the stonemasons and sculptors chiseled away, and at night oil carriers fed lamps and torches so that the work could continue without interruption.

At every stage of construction, the priestly Brahmans performed the endless rites of consecration—first purifying the building site, then tracing the initial ground plan, later crowning the superstructure with the last finial, and finally installing the principal icon in the sanctuary. When at last the project was completed, the place was charged with authority and sanctity.

As a general rule, the Hindu temple was not public. To be sure, devout individuals, most of them seeking spiritual relief in times of trouble, might come to make private offerings and recite prayers to the deity after purifying themselves with a ritual bath. But the temples had no space for a congregation to assemble, and it was generally left up to the priests to represent the community before the god. This they did with a dedicated will. Four times a day—at sunrise, noon, sunset, and midnight—a priest summoned the deity by sounding a bell and clapping his hands before entering the dark and silent sanctuary. Inside, he recited hymns to persuade Vishnu, Shiva, Kali, or another god, to enter the image before it was anointed with oils, camphor, and sandalwood. After entertaining the god with a display of moving flames, the priest offered the icon food and flowers in a manner carefully prescribed by ritual. It was thought that if in the end gods were satisfied that all the ceremonial obligations had been correctly carried out, then their pleasure would work toward the welfare and happiness of the entire community.

The temples required vast sums of money to construct and maintain—a significant part of the heavy tax burden that Indian citizens were forced to shoulder.

Economic support for the Gupta empire came largely from India's peasant villages in the form of a tax, which traditionally amounted to one-fourth of every harvest, paid directly to the royal treasury. In addition, the state required that villagers work one day each month in order to keep up its roads, tend to its wells, and expand and care for its pervasive irrigation systems. The Guptas greatly expanded agricultural acreage by constructing canals that were fed by rivers, lakes, and tanks. When the government irrigated farms, however, it usually taxed the farmers one-fiftieth of their cattle and gold, and one-sixth of their property in trees, fruit, meat, honey, and herbs. To

The Hindu deities, heroes of elaborate myths and tales, assumed many guises, as the sculptures shown here attest. On the opposite page *(left)*, Vishnu is depicted as part man, part boar, a shape that the god took when he saved the world from the sea-dwelling serpent demon. The deity is shown ascending from the ocean depths still entwined in the serpent's coils while on his shoulder sits a goddess who personifies the world. In another tale, Vishnu wore the head of a lion *(opposite page, right)* when rescuing the victims of another demon, an evil monarch named Hiranyaksipa. In the sandstone carving above, the god Shiva, second only to Vishnu in power, has been transformed into a cheerful, corpulent dwarf.

make the lot of the peasants even more woeful, the state employees who collected taxes and policed the villages frequently extorted money from them and sometimes levied illegal taxes.

Yet there was a positive side as well. Agriculture blossomed under the Guptas, providing the population with such staples as rice, wheat, and sugar. As good Hindus, Indians no longer ate much meat; cattle had become sacred, probably because they were so valuable for pulling carts and plows and providing essential foods—milk, curd, and the clarified butter called ghee, which would keep without going rancid even in the Indian heat. Fish were plentiful in many areas. India's profusion of fruits—mangoes, melons, plantains, pears, peaches, plums, pomegranates, apricots, coconuts—filled the plates of the more leisured classes. Spices such as ginger, pepper, and mustard played an important part in foreign trade.

Although agriculture dominated the Gupta economy, the government also received revenue from all salt and mineral mines, which it owned. Beyond that, the state controlled valuable tracts of land around the cities and operated various enterprises of special concern to the king, including weapons factories and gold and silver workshops. In the weaving and spinning mills they maintained to clothe the royal family and harem, the Guptas excelled in the quality of their textiles and turned a tidy profit from the export of them. (Eventually, the English language would take its terms for several kinds of cloth from Indian words and place names associated with

A part-man, part-animal deity, the elephant-headed and four-armed Ganesha is accompanied by flying attendants in this sixth century relief. Despite his grotesque shape, Ganesha, the son of Shiva and the goddess Parvati, had much power as the bestower of health, good fortune, and prosperity. His distended belly denotes refined masculine strength.

textile production and trade: calico from the southwestern port of Calicut; cashmere from mountainous Kashmir, source of that wool; chintz from *chitra,* a Sanskrit word meaning variegated.) The gold coins issued by the royal mints were works of art, and the Guptas also stamped beautiful silver, copper, bronze, and brass coins for use in the flourishing money economy of the cities.

At a time when their neighbors in Sassanian Persia were creating a top-heavy bureaucracy, the Guptas decentralized their government, handing considerable authority to village councils and permitting local landowners and military and professional people to represent their interests. Yet the price of such policy was suspicion: The Guptas operated on the theory that no official could be trusted, and they kept a watchful eye on the workings of their state through an elite corps of spies. Behind the spies, and ready to enforce the royal will, stood a strong elephant-borne army that discouraged revolt and ensured the king's control over the empire.

That control, however, was by no means absolute. As Hindu monarchs, the Guptas were bound to respect the laws of the religion, and the authority of royal edicts was, in theory at least, placed below the *Dharma Shastras,* the Brahman commentaries on those sacred laws, and the examples set by holy men, as well as the ancient hymns known as the *Vedas.* In some cases, the Hindu strictures limited the power of the king to a notable degree. He could not dispose of sacred land at will, for instance, nor could he alter any of the sacred laws. Beyond the Hindu strictures, the king was also held in check by secular laws arising from local customs and by the growth of guilds—powerful corporate associations of people who worked in a single profession or vocation. The guilds had their own written constitutions, and their decisions had the force of law among their members. As members of a particular guild, families jealously guarded the trade secrets and special techniques on which they depended for their livelihood. By passing down such knowledge orally from generation to generation, they helped preserve guild traditions—and the caste system, since particular vocations were peculiar to particular castes.

The guilds regulated even personal aspects of their members' lives, adjudicating their disputes, determining whom they might marry, and expelling those who defied their decrees. In return for the intrusive authority, the guilds offered many benefits— caring for widows and orphans, establishing fair work rules, fixing both wages and prices at reasonable levels. As it worked out, there was a good deal of team spirit about the whole process, and the guilds even had their own insignia—such as colored banners or yak tails—that the members displayed in holiday parades and at religious festivals.

The strength of the guilds reflected India's economic prosperity. A brisk internal trade in luxuries like pepper, sandalwood, coral, musk, saffron, and fine jewelry allowed caravan traders to sell their goods for three or four times the original price. From ports along India's coasts, internal commercial traffic spilled over into international trade, in which Ceylon, China, the Byzantine empire, Persia, and Arabia would come to figure prominently.

Indian merchants, accompanied by Buddhist, Jain, and Hindu missionaries, visited the far shores and river banks of the Bay of Bengal and plied the precarious South China Sea looking for spices and other trading commodities. Traveling without compasses and beset by pirates, they opened Southeast Asian markets to Indian cloth and made the southern sea route increasingly profitable. While Indian textiles, spices, jewels, ivory, and perfumes remained in demand throughout the civilized West—in

Egypt, Greece, and Rome—Indian ships also sailed south to Ceylon, then swept east through the Malacca Straits to Southeast Asia, where Chinese merchant vessels would exchange musk, raw silk, and amber for cotton, ivory, and even elephants.

There, in Burma, Sumatra, Java, Malaya, Siam, and Funan (the land that eventually would be called Cambodia), an informal socio-geographical entity known as Greater India came into being. Local states and royal courts, having made contact with India through its merchants and missionaries, sought to import Indian civilization wholesale, at first slavishly imitating its court life and its religions, with all their elaborate accouterments. They became prosperous Hindu or Buddhist kingdoms, some of them, such as Funan, run by Brahmans, others influenced by wealthy merchants who had married into local ruling families.

Yet despite the expanding overseas interests, domestic spending in India on increasingly expensive public projects led to high interest rates, inflation, and widespread bankruptcy. The Guptas devoted much attention to debtors, and a growing body of Hindu law focused on the appropriate punishments for those who failed to pay what they owed. In addition to the punishment they received during their lifetimes, debtors were promised further chastisement in the hereafter—while the unexpunged debt was passed on to their legal heirs. The penalties were significantly lighter for the Brahman and warrior classes than for the majority living in India's villages.

Thus, the Indian villager—laboring under heavy taxes, plagued by debt, his existence circumscribed by caste and regulated by government, religion, and guild— drank a good deal of wine, turned to his family for solace, and prayed for nothing so much as a good marriage and fine sons. Daily life revolved around the family, and men dominated Indian families. Hindu law prescribed eight kinds of marriage, each carrying its own set of rules and obligations. They ranged from weddings that began with abduction and rape to those that resulted from purchase or family arrangements to perfect love matches. A man could wed as many wives as he wanted, but most marriages were monogamous.

Although Hindu men sometimes forced their wives into seclusion, most women enjoyed a certain amount of freedom, albeit restricted. They bathed in the rivers and attended various ceremonies in the houses of their neighbors and relatives. During religious celebrations, marriage ceremonies, spring festivals, and holidays, women might well be found attending dramatic performances, taking pleasure baths in public tanks, and drinking wine along with the men. (In fact, Indian men thought intoxication lent special charm to women.) Although a woman who committed adultery with a man of lower caste was utterly reviled, and sometimes torn apart by dogs, a woman who strayed with a man of higher caste got off relatively easily. She was required to wear dirty clothes and sleep on the ground until her next menstrual period, after which she resumed her normal place in the home and her husband's bed.

Women whose husbands were rich enough to afford jewelry bedecked themselves with an array of precious stones and metals. Many persuaded their husbands to invest a sizable share of the family capital in their own personal adornment. There was good reason for this acquisitive behavior: A woman needed to have as much wealth as she could possibly accumulate, since Hindu laws were particularly harsh on widows. With rare exceptions, a widow was not permitted to inherit her husband's real estate—only movable property, such as jewels. Widows were required to be celibate, and they were banned from most kinds of ceremonies, including weddings. Some Hindu lawgivers recommended that widows should voluntarily cast themselves on the funeral pyres of their husbands in a rite known as suttee, and a surprising number actually followed that brutal advice, some of them under duress from the families of their late husbands.

When Chandra Gupta II died in 415, his son Kumara Gupta came to the throne. The latter ruled for forty years of general peace and prosperity, but the empire that he turned over intact to his son Skanda Gupta was menaced by the White Huns, who were making their first fierce attempts to breach the Khyber Pass. Skanda Gupta, the last great king of his dynasty, put up a valiant but vain defense against the Hunnish onslaughts. By the time of his death in 467, the royal treasury had been bled dry by war and the end of the empire was in sight.

The White Huns took the Punjab before the year 500, then Kashmir and most of the Ganges plain. By the middle of the sixth century they had shattered the last of the resistence. And India, its imperial glory vanished, its economy destroyed, its politics fragmented, degenerated once again into a disputatious collection of small kingdoms.

Meanwhile, during its period of subservience to the White Huns, Sassanian Persia had suffered its own discomforts. The White Huns required heavy tribute payments and intervened openly in Sassanian domestic affairs, including making sure a pliable king sat on the Persian throne. Peroz's defeat had been followed by near collapse of the Persian economy and widespread famine. Toward the end of the fifth century, the troubled times gave rise to a new religious heresy clearly aimed at causing political and social upheaval.

Its founder was a former priest of the Magi named Mazdak, and his creed, a primitive communism, demanded not only that the granaries of the nobles be opened to the entire community but also that aristocrats should give up a few of their many wives and concubines to the peasants. In better days, Mazdakism would surely have received short shrift, but in a country impoverished by many years of war, it held wide appeal—and was, incredibly, supported by even the Sassanian king Kavadh. For this behavior, Kavadh was deposed by a coalition of nobles and the Magi, and fled to refuge with the White Huns, who restored him to his throne. But he had learned his lesson about challenging the Persian establishment: He had Mazdak murdered and viciously purged the heretic's followers.

The eccentric Kavadh was succeeded by his son Chosroes I, a vigorous and astute ruler who would lead the empire in a resurgence to former glories. When yet another warlike Asian people, the Turks, appeared for the first time on the Iranian horizon, Chosroes married their leader's daughter and persuaded them to join him in driving out the White Huns—which they proceeded to do with ferocious gusto.

At home, Chosroes streamlined the Sassanian administration, imposed reforms on the tax system, reorganized the army, and revived the mystical majesty of the throne, embellishing his court with luxuries of which old Ardashir could hardly have dreamed. He topped his palace with the largest iwans ever constructed and affected a crown so heavy with gold that it had to be suspended on chains to keep it from breaking his regal neck.

Once again, Persia was ready to do battle on its western front, and the wars begun by Chosroes against Byzantium would continue for another century. Not until the middle of the seventh century would the Sassanian dynasty finally fall—and then not to Roman legions or Asian barbarians, but to a power making its first appearance on the world stage—Arabs united and energized by the new religion of Islam.

Inspired by the dazzling artistic achievements of the Gupta empire to the north, sculptors in southern India created one of the greatest of all Hindu monuments at Mamallapuram, a coastal town thirty miles south of Madras. There teams of artisans hewed a series of monolithic temples *(below)* and from a large granite outcropping carved the huge, magnificent bas-relief shown at right. Multitudes are represented—mortals, deities, and animals—most of them hastening toward a vertical cleft in the center of the rock that represents the River Ganges, to give thanks for its life-giving waters. According to Hindu myth, the earth originally lacked water but then, in part through the intercession of the great god Shiva, the Ganges flowed down from the firmament to make its headwaters in the Himalayas. All the figures in the relief are life-size, including the massive family of elephants at far right.

CHINESE KINGDOMS IN TURMOIL

3 Many centuries after the era of conquests, historians would comment upon the similarities that marked the collapse of the two great empires situated at opposite ends of the Eurasian landmass. In China as in Rome, hordes of barbarians descended from the north, a new religion stirred waves of spiritual fervor, and the breakup of imperial authority produced rival empires.

Yet these similarities turned out to be less profound than the differences. In the West, the glitter of Rome faded into a memory, but the Chinese struggled—through four centuries of political upheaval and armed conflict—toward an imperial glory that would outshine all past eastern empires. Without totally transforming their society, they absorbed the alien religion that challenged them, and unlike the Romans, they assimilated the foreign invaders who split their nation. China emerged from its conflicts with the empire not merely restored but strengthened.

The old empire of the Han dynasty fell apart through a combination of weak rulers, court intrigue, and rebellion. Its collapse, which dated from the death in AD 189 of the last uncontested Han emperor, Lingdi, threw China into virtual anarchy. Contending generals waged civil war, and armed bands pillaged the countryside. Peasants took refuge on the fortified estates of big landowners, exchanging their freedom and that of their descendants for protection and economic security. Trade languished. As copper production fell, coins became scarce, because people either hoarded them or melted them down to use the metal. The money economy ground almost to a halt; rudimentary barter became the primary medium of exchange.

In 220, after more than three decades of turmoil, the country's most powerful warlords established a measure of stability. They began dividing the old empire into three kingdoms whose boundaries were determined by the regions where the warlords were strongest. Each kingdom was ruled by a newly founded royal house: the Wei in the north, the Wu in the south, and the Shu in the west. Even then, with the launching of the period to be known as the Three Kingdoms, the hold of the Han legacy was so strong that each ruler declared himself the rightful imperial heir, and each sought to enforce his claim by warring on the others.

Their claims varied in validity. The Wu, in their new homeland south of the Yangtze River, had no historic ties to the Han throne at all. To the west, in the region that was to become the province of Sichuan, the Shu leader, Liu Bei, was a distant descendant of the Han clan and bore the same family name. The Wei in the north possessed a different kind of imperial connection. They were descended from a gifted warlord, poet, and military strategist named Cao Cao, who during the decline of the Han dynasty had served as protector of a figurehead emperor named Xiandi, successor to Lingdi. Xiandi ruled in name only: Cao Cao pulled the strings. In 220, after Cao Cao's death, the puppet was forced to abdicate. He formally abolished the Han dynasty and ceded the throne to his late protector's son, Cao Pei, who thereupon proclaimed the Wei dynasty.

Cao Pei and his Wei successors backed up their claim to legitimacy with the power that grew out of controlling the ancient Chinese heartland. This agricultural and historic core of empire was centered in the North China plain, a fertile, 125,000-square-mile stretch of alluvial earth nourished by the Yellow River. The Wei had not only the richest lands, but the most people—according to one census of the era about 29 million, compared with 11 million in Wu and 7 million in Shu. The north also kept the largest royal court to bolster the Wei claim that they, like the Han, should rule all of China. They employed in their capital, Luoyang, a corps of officials so enormous it could have staffed the Han dynasty at its peak.

The Wei were in fact determined to restore to China a strong central government. To this end, they rebuilt their army—originally a hodgepodge of mercenaries and former bandits—around a professional core of mounted archers from nomadic tribes that had settled in northern China. And to ensure a steady stream of recruits, they instituted a special class of families to provide professional soldiers. Members, identified and registered as military families, were allowed to marry only within that class.

The Wei also revived agriculture, which had been crippled by the civil wars. Drainage and irrigation works were built. Agricultural colonies, where dispossessed peasants and soldier-farmers were given tools and animals and put to work for the state, were instituted. These colonies, some of which employed tens of thousands of men, strengthened Wei outlying defenses while stimulating the moribund economy.

In strengthening the sinews of the state, the Wei sought to curb the growing power of the northern aristocracy. With its

Following the collapse of the Han dynasty in AD 220, China underwent four centuries of political chaos and warfare. Barbarians called Huns invaded from Mongolia and took over the Chinese heartland in the Yellow River valley, sending a million refugees fleeing to the sparsely settled territory south of the Yangtze River. During this period of flight and confusion, warlords throughout China founded many short-lived kingdoms. Not until the year 589 was the country reunified by a dynasty known as the Sui.

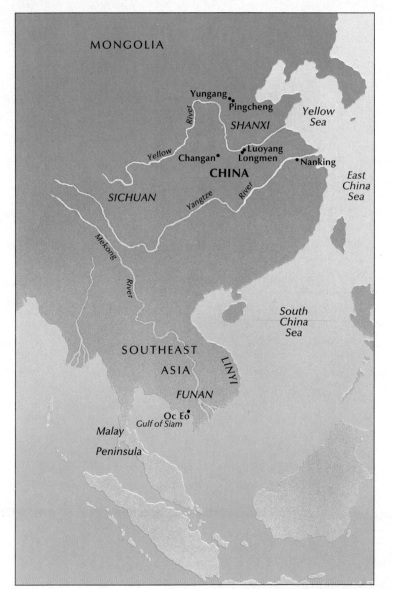

Scores of miniature warriors—such as this earthenware cavalryman—that were entombed with a Chinese nobleman testify to the near-constant state of warfare that existed in China between the collapse of the Han dynasty early in the third century and the ascent of the Sui late in the sixth century. Both horse and rider shown here are wearing traditional fighting garb—flexible leather armor designed to blunt the force of arrows.

history of hereditary privilege, this class of wealthy landowners was an elite group of perhaps a few dozen families with several hundred adult males each. Sheltered on fortified estates and protected by private armies, they had prospered and grown stronger during the chaotic decades after the fall of the Han. They extended their estates by appropriating territory and by absorbing into service the peasants who had lost their own land, both to the vagaries of war and to the encroachments of the aristocracy that now enthralled them. Some estates were nearly as large as the government-established agricultural colonies, serving as home to more than 10,000 slaves, serfs, and clients. The purses of the rich were so swollen with the fruits of civil war that one land baron was able to provide his daughter with a bridal dowry of "1,000 slave girls sumptuously garbed in silk."

The dispersal of so much power and wealth among the aristocracy posed the threat that China, like Europe after the collapse of the Roman Empire, might disintegrate into a loose conglomeration of independent autonomous feudal estates. But the aristocrats' desire for prestigious court positions helped counter their tendency to become alienated from central authority. In fact, their very success in dominating high civil and military posts created a different kind of problem: The aristocrats did not want to eliminate centralized power; they simply wished to control the empire themselves.

To limit the aristocracy's role in the government bureaucracy, the Wei established a system intended to select officials for ability rather than family. Put into effect at the beginning of the dynasty in 220, the system was called *jiupin zhongzheng*—nine ranks impartial and just. Local magistrates from the upper class were charged with the responsibility of gathering information about prospective candidates for office from their neighborhoods. The magistrates ranked candidates according to estimates of character and ability. Rank determined the level of entry into the government, which in turn had bearing on how high one could rise.

More successful in conquering external enemies than in bringing the great families to heel, the Wei army inflicted several defeats on the Shu to the west, finally subjugating that kingdom in 263. By that time, however, the aristocracy had gained control of the Wei government, using as one of its instruments the nine-ranks system intended to keep the upper classes in line. The aristocratic magistrates ignored ability and assigned ranks to candidates on the basis of family wealth and prestige.

In 265, two years after the defeat of Shu, a member of one of the great families put an end to the Wei dynasty. Sima Yan, son and grandson of generals, usurped the throne and founded the new Jin dynasty. In 280, his army subdued the southern state of Wu, uniting all three kingdoms once again under one government.

Sima Yan's remaining decade on the Jin throne was a time of prosperity and stability. He undid much of the work of the Wei that had strengthened the central government—putting an end to the agricultural colonies, for example, and establishing an academy to train young nobles for top government positions. He distributed power generously, perhaps recklessly, to his family. No fewer than twenty-seven of his kinsmen were given large fiefdoms. Each could appoint officials, keep a private army of up to 5,000 men, and pocket tax revenues from peasants.

His new Jin court in Luoyang now became the capital of all China, and emissaries from numerous countries flocked there. In 284, the emperor received representatives bearing gifts even from as far as the Roman Empire. Among the representatives paying homage to the Jin were two from a pair of young kingdoms much closer to home, in Southeast Asia: Funan, centered on the lower reaches of the Mekong River in what eventually became Cambodia; and Linyi, or Champa, which occupied the long narrow strip of territory to the east that one day would be known as Vietnam. Both of these southern kingdoms had been established before the third century by colonists from India. The Chinese periodically fought with Champa over contested border areas and over acts of piracy by that nation's infamous mariners. But the main focus of Chinese interest to the south was Funan, an important way station on the maritime route from the Mediterranean through Southeast Asia to China.

Funan's port, Oc Eo, was situated three miles from the Gulf of Siam and linked to it by a network of canals. Canals laced the city, which was composed largely of houses erected on piles, and formed part of a larger web of waterways that stretched for more than 125 miles. Originally constructed to drain swampy regions, these canals also irrigated rice fields, and the largest were navigable by seagoing ships as far inland as China. So extensive was the system that Chinese travelers plying the canals en route to the Malay Peninsula spoke of "sailing across Funan."

The first official Chinese emissaries to Funan arrived there about 230, during the period of the Three Kingdoms. Representing the southern kingdom of Wu, which was blocked by the Wei from the overland route across Central Asia to the West, they wanted to open up a maritime connection. One of the emissaries, Kang Tai, provided the first known Chinese written account of life in Funan. He wrote approvingly of the kingdom's walled villages and palaces and its books and writing, which resembled a script of Indian origin. But he noted with some scorn that the men "go about naked." He persuaded the king, Fan Xun, to issue a decree ordering men to cover themselves. As a result, the citizens began wearing a piece of cloth wrapped around the waist, a garment that would evolve into the traditional Cambodian *sampot*.

Some years later, a Chinese visitor to Funan's neighbor Champa reported on the exotic rituals surrounding that country's royal court: "The king wears a tall hat decorated with gold flowers and trimmed with a silk tassel. When he goes out he mounts an elephant; he is preceded by conchs and drums, sheltered under a parasol, and surrounded by servants who wave banners."

Under the Jin, Funan, Champa, and other nations sent envoys to Luoyang, men whose presence marked the high point of the dynasty's ascendancy over a temporarily united China. Unity was short-lived, however. When the dynasty's founder, Sima Yan, died in 290, the empire plunged once more into chaos. Sima Yan himself had helped set the stage for anarchy a decade before his death. After the conquest of the Wu in the south, he had decreed a general disarmament in order to reduce costs and restore men to the ranks of the tax-paying peasantry. Soldiers of the central government were sent home and ordered to surrender their arms. The idea was to melt down the arms in order to mint money, which was in such short supply that officials had to be paid with grain and silks in lieu of coin. But the majority of the discharged soldiers kept their weapons and later sold them to the highest bidders, usually northern barbarian peoples such as the Xiongnu and Xianbei, often in exchange for land. Meanwhile, in the provinces, the imperial relatives on whom Sima Yan had bestowed a great deal of power refused to disarm at all, insisting they needed their armies as personal bodyguards.

The struggle for the throne that followed the death of Sima Yan was waged in large part with these private armies. Rival clans challenged the imperial family, and for six fratricidal years beginning in 301, Sima Yan's own relatives, including three sons, fought one another from their bases throughout the north. One prince would seize the

A smiling civil official wearing the cylindrical cap of an aristocratic courtier rests on his ceremonial sword. Such bureaucratic attendants were usually members of old and established families; a man of humble origin might occasionally rise high in governmental service, but he would be shunned by the social elite.

throne by assassinating his brother, the incumbent, only to fall to the blade of another ambitious brother. The fighting coincided with a devastating series of natural calamities: flood and drought, locusts and plague.

During this time of frightful insecurity, there was a revival of interest in the school of thought known as Taoism, or Daoism, whose principles had been set forth in the sixth century BC by the sage Laozi. More than 700 years later, Daoism had been transformed into a popular religion by an infusion of magic, alchemy, and other practices introduced by priests and faith healers, who came to the fore as society was in upheaval. In those troubled times, the new religion offered much that the predominant philosophy and ethical code, Confucianism, could not. Confucianism, rooted in the principle of stable government and harmony between rulers and subjects, was losing its influence. It had failed to prevent anarchy, and in any event, it was too earthbound to satisfy the spiritual yearnings of many people. Confucian doctrine advocated respect for the spirits but urged that they be kept at a distance.

By contrast, religious Daoism held out the promise of long life and even immortality. To achieve these goals, the adherent was urged to follow the Dao, or Way, by a prescribed course of conduct that might range from meditation upon the teachings of the master Laozi, to special breathing exercises and the use of drugs, to communing with nature, confessing sins, and doing good deeds. Daoism took many forms. In the second century, for instance, Daoist groups were strong and well defined; they launched rebellions against the Han during the 180s that raged for nearly three decades and helped hasten the fall of the empire. After the suppression of these revolts, however, the idea of a centralized movement disappeared and popular Daoism flourished only at the local level.

During the third and fourth centuries, Daoism exerted a more lasting influence. One Daoist cult, for example, focused on inner hygiene. The practitioner had to give up wine, meat, and cereals and undertake arduous breathing exercises. The result, according to the cult, was to cleanse the three "cinnabar fields" in the body, nurture the 36,000 internal gods, and suppress the three worms that caused disease, old age, and death. Some of the cult's ideas about diet and breathing would survive the centuries to persist in modern-day China.

Daoism also influenced science and art. A branch of Daoism experimented with alchemy—the attempt to convert base metals into gold—in search of a life-prolonging elixir. These experiments led to the development of new medicines and other chemicals. In the process, the Daoist alchemists undoubtedly sampled all sorts of organic and inorganic substances, a practice that probably contributed to the richness of Chinese culinary art—and to the death by poisoning of some who sampled the elixirs. At the same time, Daoist ideas about the potential harmony of nature and the human spirit exerted a profound impact on poetry and painting. Inspired by Daoism, landscape painting—the Chinese called it "mountain and water" painting—emerged more than a millennium before its appearance in Europe.

With its promise of serenity, the movement lured many intellectuals away from government at a time when these men were desperately needed. "I am hoping to ascend a famous mountain where I will regulate my diet and cultivate my nature," wrote Gong He, a highborn soldier who turned to Daoism early in the fourth century. "It is not that I wish to abandon worldly affairs, but unless I do so, how can I practice the abstruse and tranquil Way?"

Turning away from the political turbulence, learned men such as Gong He gathered to engage in metaphysical speculation, developing witty and refined discussions that came to be called *qingtan*—pure conversations. Among the best-known gatherings were those held by a third-century group of wealthy and eccentric recluses who met in a scenic spot near the capital, Luoyang. Styling themselves the Seven Sages of the Bamboo Grove, they debated philosophy, composed poetry, played the lute, drank too much wine, and extolled the virtues of political inaction.

The withdrawal from public life of men such as the Seven Sages both symbolized and contributed to the breakdown of society during the last years of the Jin dynasty in Luoyang. It was one more factor—together with corruption, drought, and other natural calamities, and the incessant fighting among families and within them—that paved the way for China's most tumultuous event of the fourth century: the take-over of the northern realm of the newly reunited empire by alien peoples.

The Chinese referred to these peoples as the Five Barbarians. Nomads of varying ethnicity, the invaders included two groups of sheep breeders who had originated in the area of Tibet, to the northwest. Three other groups were cattle raisers and raiders from the steppes to the north, the country later to be called Mongolia. Many of these foreigners already lived within the northern Chinese border or just beyond. They had been moving into China for over two centuries with the permission, even encouragement, of officials who wanted them as soldiers and conscript laborers and sometimes sold them as slaves. By the end of the third century, they were so numerous that in one region, around the old northwestern capital of Changan, they made up about half of the estimated population of one million.

The barbarians took advantage of the anarchy gripping northern China at the beginning of the fourth century to further infiltrate and invade the country. Several groups even set up their own separatist regimes on Chinese soil. The most powerful of these alien governments was established in 304 in the border province of Shanxi by the tribes of the Xiongnu, former Mongolian nomads who spoke a language of Turkic origin. The Xiongnu were also known to Chinese as the Hu and to westerners as Huns. These nomads were almost certainly distant cousins of the notorious Huns of Attila who descended upon Europe and the Roman Empire during the fifth century.

The Chinese Huns, however, were a far cry from their brethren, whose name became equated with terrorism. Many of the Xiongnu had already adopted Chinese ways and had served in the Jin armies, where they were valued for their horsemanship and archery skill. They had even supplied generals for Chinese forces. Many of the farmers who produced food for the Huns in Shanxi were former Chinese soldiers who had traded their weapons to the Huns for land and prospered in the relative stability that prevailed in Xiongnu territories. Even disaffected Chinese gentry had come north to be teachers and political advisers for the Hun nobility.

The Huns were so sinicized, in fact, that they named their new state in Shanxi the Kingdom of Han. This bent toward Chinese culture was pushed by the charismatic Hun leader Liu Yuan, who as a boy had been taken hostage by the Chinese and made a page at the imperial court in Luoyang. He understood the basics of Chinese government and history and could read the classical texts. His court in southern Shanxi was based on the Chinese model. When Liu Yuan proclaimed himself emperor in 308 and launched a rebellion against the tottering Jin dynasty, he declared himself a legitimate successor to the Han rulers of all China. He even cited evidence to uphold his claim. He pointed out that a distant Hun ancestor, who 500 years before had concluded a peace treaty with the first Han emperor, had married Chinese

Displaying valor and loyalty, a concubine named Lady Feng helps royal guards to ward off a circus bear that had threatened Emperor Yuan *(right)*.

omen who were members of the Chinese upper classes played a privileged but restricted role in the rigidly structured social hierarchy. Emperors, ministers, and courtiers usually had numerous concubines in addition to a wife, and all were expected to adhere to the traditional rules of etiquette governed by a well-defined code of conduct called the *Nü shi zhen tu,* or *Admonitions and Instructions for Court Ladies.* The *Admonitions* were initially recorded in the third century by Zhang Hua, a poet who was disturbed by what he perceived to be a lack of decorum on the part of the empress and her retinue.

Some 100 years later, an artist named Gu Kaizhi transcribed a portion of the *Admonitions* in a delicately rendered scroll painting. A copy of Gu's scroll, which was made during the Tang dynasty, appears here and on the following pages, accompanied by excerpts from the courtly instructions.

COURTLY RULES OF CONDUCT

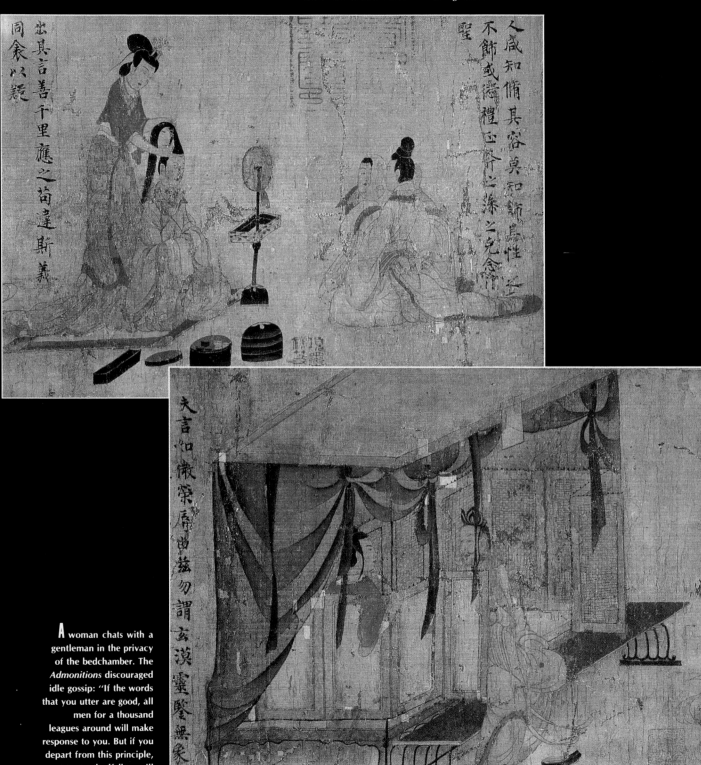

One imperial concubine combs the hair of another, while a third court lady paints her eyebrows in the popular fashion. "Women know how to adorn their faces," the instruction reads in part; "yet if the character be not adorned, there is a danger that the rules of conduct may be transgressed."

A woman chats with a gentleman in the privacy of the bedchamber. The *Admonitions* discouraged idle gossip: "If the words that you utter are good, all men for a thousand leagues around will make response to you. But if you depart from this principle, even your bedfellow will distrust you."

Wives of the court oversee a tutorial session for two children. Women were expected to fulfill their domestic duties: "Do not let your fancies roam afar," advised the *Admonitions*.

The Imperial Instructress pens her admonitions to the ladies of the court, as two concubines look on. "Therefore I say, be watchful," she writes, "keep an eager guard over your behavior, thence happiness will come. Fulfill your duties calmly and respectfully, reflect before you act. Then you shall win glory and honor."

princesses. Moreover, Liu Yuan's own family bore the imperial Han surname, Liu.

None of these tenuous Chinese connections served to lessen the barbarity of the warfare that ensued. One of Liu Yuan's generals, a headstrong former slave named Shi Le, wrought havoc when he swept across the northeastern provinces in 310. He and his horde of Huns resumed the tribal practice of making surprise raids rather than waging pitched battles. In these attacks, they killed more than 100,000 Chinese—among them forty-eight princes of the Jin dynasty waiting in a vast funeral procession for the burial of a fellow prince. Liu died that year, but by 316 the Huns and other northern tribes that had been infiltrating the region since the time of the Wei controlled all of northern China, the homeland of Chinese civilization. Despair at China's plight ran so deep that it affected even foreign traders who now inhabited the larger cities. A Sogdian merchant named Nanai Vandak wrote his employer in Samarkand this plaintive note: "And, Sir, if I wrote you all the details of how China fared, it would be a story of debts and woe. You will have no wealth from it."

In another incarnation, however, the Jin dynasty survived. South of the Yangtze River, at a city that later would be called Nanking (literally, Southern Capital), but which was then named Jiankang, one of the Jin Sima family princes restored the dynasty. In 317, he declared himself the first emperor of what was to be known as the Eastern Jin dynasty and took the name Yuandi. China was now split into two realms separated by an ill-defined border running east and west through the upper Yangtze Valley. This division would persist for over two and a half centuries, with North China being torn into fragments by rival groups of barbarians, and South China remaining intact under the ethnic Chinese who poured down from the north.

An estimated one million Chinese fled south during the first quarter of the fourth century to escape the barbarians, the famines, and Jin internecine warfare. They found in the south a sharply different physical environment, a lush semitropical region that, unlike the north, was green most of the year. Except for the fertile lower Yangtze Valley, which was the site of the capital, Jiankang, the entire region tended to be sparsely settled. It was populated largely by indigenous non-Chinese peoples such as the Tai (whose descendants in Southeast Asia would be called the Thai), but governed by the Chinese who had emigrated there from northern China about a century before to establish the short-lived kingdom of Wu.

Among the new refugees were many aristocrats who had helped rule the north into ruin. At first, they fought with the old established families of the south, who, although they were Chinese, spoke different dialects and had developed different customs. Such differences were officially recognized in the colors of the tax registers—white for the northerners, yellow for the original residents.

But the aristocratic newcomers, in collaboration with the richest of the old-line colonial familes, soon came to dominate the south as they had the north. They controlled the economy, monopolized high office, and made and unmade a succession of weak emperors. Many members of the great northern clans in exile gravitated to Jiankang to grab power in the Eastern Jin dynasty. Jiankang, already a major trade center, enjoyed tremendous growth and glorification as the new capital. In 318 alone, some 200,000 officials were appointed to the government. Some aristocrats settled outside the city on large tax-exempt estates granted by the emperor—tracts that had been common land where villagers had gathered firewood and grazed their animals. The rich turned these plots into manors with fruit plantations, vegetable gardens and hot houses, bamboo groves and parks stocked with exotic animals. They created artificial streams and ponds and constructed and landscaped artificial mountains. Some of their houses were cooled by elaborate water systems.

Still yearning for their lost homeland, immigrants from the north gave transplanted place names to new areas that they settled. They learned to produce rice instead of the wheat and millet that had been the staples in the cooler climate and less fertile soil of the north. They also learned to grow the shrub with fragrant white flowers that yielded what one day would be China's national drink. The Chinese may have begun drinking tea before the third century, but the earliest surviving references to it were written then. The bush was cultivated in the south; the brew would not come into general use in the north for four or five centuries. Only the richest of the southern families could afford the rarest and best tea leaves—the kind, as described breathlessly by a Chinese author a couple of centuries later, that would "curl like the dewlap of a mighty bullock, unfold like a mist rising out of a ravine, gleam like a lake touched by a zephyr, and be wet and soft like fine earth newly swept by rain."

Family status became so important in the south that the study of genealogy flowered as never before. Families needed pedigrees to make clear their eligibility for high office or for marriage to the highborn. Books on the bloodlines of the most eminent families began to appear under such names as Register of the One Hundred Clans. The government even established a special bureau of genealogy, employing scholars to research ancestry and weed out fraudulent claims.

Aristocrats often went to absurd lengths to distance themselves from those of lesser pedigree. According to one story, a high government official would place his guests near him, on the finely woven and embroidered mats used for seating in the homes of leading families. But he would then order the servants to move his own mat away from any guests he considered his inferiors. For all the snobbery, however, the old custom of concubinage ensured that the bloodlines of aristocracy and peasantry would merge—to the genetic enrichment of both.

The old nine-ranks system of grading candidates for government office had been brought south to ensure aristocratic control of the bureaucracy. Nearly 75 percent of the highest Eastern Jin officials belonged to great clans such as the Wang, the Yu, and the Huan. These families constituted what was virtually a self-perpetuating oligarchy. A scholar of the era contrasted this with the earlier times in which "what a man knew and how he acted were most important." But now, the scholar went on, government officials "lord it over each other and squabble about trifles; what they discuss is always family; they never talk about virtue or ability."

The estates of the great families were the focal points of much of southern cultural life. They attracted poets, painters, scholars, and musicians and dancers. The arts thrived. For the first time, artists painted images of the physical world about them, establishing the landscape as a great Chinese artistic tradition. Calligraphy, the art of beautiful handwriting, also came into its own now. But the most notable achievements were in poetry. Many of China's best known poets wrote during this era, and verse was so popular among the southern gentry that it became a kind of party game for their salons. The host would set the challenge with a five-syllable or seven-syllable line, and guests would compete to see who could supply the best completion for the poem, obeying standard rhyme scheme, length, and meter.

Most artists were contemptuous of the Chinese who stayed in the north under barbarian rulers, and were convinced that their own work constituted true Chinese culture. Northern literature was dismissed by a southern poet as nothing more than

"the braying of donkeys and the barking of dogs." In addition, the salons of the émigré aristocracy often featured that peculiar Daoist institution brought from the north—qingtan, or pure conversation. Now, however, instead of focusing on the metaphysics of Daoism, the discussion increasingly centered on the doctrines of a foreign religion that was slowly gaining in popularity: Buddhism.

Founded in India about 500 BC, Buddhism was introduced into China some 600 years later. It was brought by foreign merchants and others traveling the overland trade routes and the sea-lanes that led into Southeast Asia. The missionaries who followed them established a few monastic communities in large cities. From there, the new faith, whose main tenets seemed to contradict the deepest characteristics and ideals of the Chinese people, took hold very slowly. To begin with, many Chinese considered anything of foreign origin to be inherently inferior. More important, Buddhism's emphasis on immortality through reincarnation and its tragic view of life ran counter to the traditional Chinese preoccupation with the here and now. And the requirement of celibacy for Buddhist monks was contrary to the Chinese love of family and children. Even the tonsure—the ritual shaving of the monk's head—violated Confucian tradition, which held that altering the body in such a way constituted disrespect for the parents who had provided it.

But like Daoism, Buddhism benefited from the turbulence of the times. To people yearning for relief from incessant fighting, it offered the appeal of the peaceful monastic life and the prospect of personal salvation. For the educated, Buddhism provided a stimulating new set of ideas. To the common folk, it promised much of the same faith healing and magic that made Daoism attractive, while adding an intriguing host of deities and a hierarchy of heavens and hells.

Chinese suspicion and then acceptance of Buddhism were represented in the old story told about Sun Hao, the last emperor of Wu, whose reign ended in 280. The emperor was so contemptuous of Buddhism, the story goes, that he had to be talked out of destroying the few temples the sect had managed to build in his land. When a Buddhist image was excavated in an imperial park, he had it moved to a urinal. There, to the amusement of his courtiers, he personally performed what he mockingly called "the washing of the Buddha." But he was immediately struck down by a mysterious, painful disease—and recovered, it was said, only after he accepted the new religion and ordered all his courtiers to adore the Buddha.

Old tales aside, Buddhism began to find widespread favor during the following century in both north and south. In the south, practice of the religion spread from the top of society down (unlike Christianity in the Roman Empire, which took root first among the masses). It gained impetus from the upper classes, who discussed Buddhist doctrine in pure-conversation sessions. And its popularity among the elite rose as aristocrats entered the priesthood. These gentleman monks could move comfortably through the salons of the great families, where they preached a Chinese version of Buddhism in terms understandable to their aristocratic colleagues.

Through one of the great families, the Wangs from Langye, Buddhism became entrenched at the imperial court in Jiankang. In the years after the exodus to the south, the most influential members of this clan were the cousins Wang Dao and Wang Dun. Wang Dun's younger brother, who was referred to as the "gen-

Imposing but serene, Buddha *(far left)* offers a blessing as two disciples stand in attendance. The cliffside cave temple at Tun Huang, which houses the shrine shown here, is part of an elaborate Buddhist complex, which attests to the important role of religion in the Northern Zhou and Sui dynasties. The figures were molded from a mixture of mud, straw, and camel dung; then they were coated with clay, whitewashed, and brightly painted, as were walls of the cave itself.

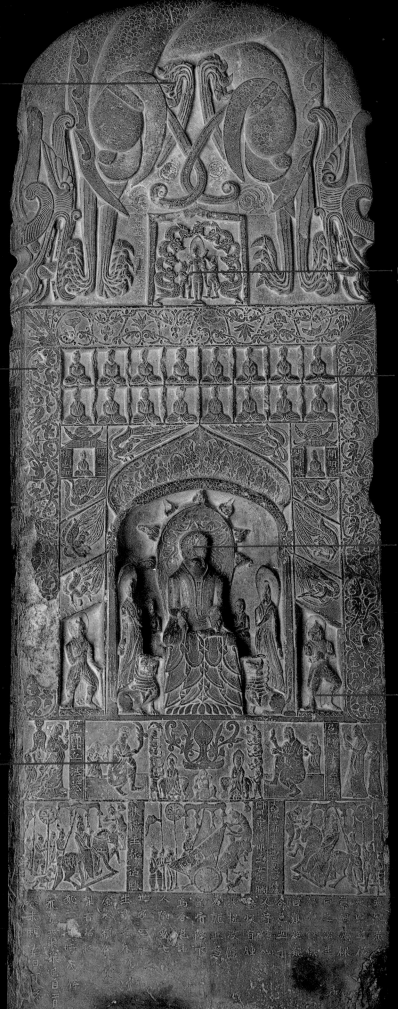

The monument is crowned by the figures of six intertwined dragons, symbolic bearers of good luck.

Buddha is being born in this symbolic portrayal.

The border of the central panel is an interlocking pattern of dragons and flowers, indicative of power and fertility.

Two rows of meditating Buddhas evoke the divinity's numerous earthly incarnations.

The enthroned Buddha is flanked by two bodhisattvas—semidivine disciples—and guarded by two lions, symbolic defenders of the faith.

These stylized portraits of two Buddhist monks are representative of the authority of the church.

Several of the more important donors of the monument are shown bearing gifts to a Buddhist temple.

tleman from beyond the world," served as a kind of court chaplain. His most prominent convert was Mingdi, the second emperor in the Eastern Jin dynasty and evidently the first Chinese monarch to outspokenly champion the new faith. Soon, the shaved heads and saffron robes of monks were a familiar sight at the Eastern Jin court. (Nuns also became a common sight at court toward the end of the fourth century; not infrequently, they were highborn widows or survivors of a dead prince's harem.)

Monks not only preached at court but sometimes acted as unofficial advisers to the sovereign in secular matters. On occasion, an emperor would ask a monk to leave the priesthood to serve as a high government official. Such requests created a dilemma—and sometimes a risk. One Chinese governor ordered a monk to return to secular life in his service and when the monk refused, had him whipped to death.

Priests, even those at court, strove to maintain their independence. This concept was new to the Chinese, whose traditional court religion was bound up with imperial authority. The issue of Buddhist autonomy often hinged upon the question of whether monks should pay their respects to earthly rulers by bowing down before the throne as others did. In 403, the southern emperor referred the matter to one of the most venerable of monks, Huiyuan, who was then nearing seventy. The priest's courageous answer, accepted by the emperor, was contained in the title of a treatise he wrote a few months later: "A Monk Does Not Bow Down before a King."

By 420, when the rule of the Eastern Jin dynasty came to an end, the south had no fewer than 1,768 monasteries and 24,000 monks and nuns. The last Jin ruler, Emperor Gong, was one of the most devout. In 420, Gong was forced to abdicate by Liu Yu, a general who had won power and popularity through victorious campaigns against the north. The new monarch ordered his predecessor killed in the time-honored way—by "voluntarily" taking poison. But when the guards offered Gong the vial, he refused it, saying: "The Buddha teaches that he who commits suicide cannot return to a human body." The guards smothered him with a bedcover.

Gong's brave death ended a dynasty that had endured for slightly longer than a century. Jerked about by the great families, many of the Eastern Jin emperors were mere puppets; several of them were still children when they were placed on the throne. Of the eleven emperors, only four reigned longer than six years. Most of the others' careers were cut short by coups and assassination. Toward the end of the dynasty, power passed to the military and local warlords, although socially predominant families remained in the aristocracy. The ascendancy of the soldiers, many of whom belonged to private armies beyond central government control, did little for stability. Four new dynasties were installed during the 170-year period after the Eastern Jin. Each was begun by a general of obscure background who usurped the throne amid bloody intrigue, and each ended in much the same way.

The most stable and notable reign during this post-Jin period belonged to Emperor Wu, who founded the Liang dynasty in 502. In the early years, Wu presided over a time of peace and prosperity. He reformed the nine-rank system to undermine traditional upper-class political clout, which was in the process of being even more thoroughly shaken by the rise to power of merchants grown wealthy from domestic commerce and foreign trade in the cities along the Yangtze. He decreed in 509 that "all those with talent may advance along the road of success" and set an example by promoting his personal servant, who later became his most successful general.

Though Wu himself was a former general who had seized the throne by force, he became best known as a zealous Buddhist. He forsook his family's old religion,

This intricately carved limestone monolith was erected in AD 529 as an imposing memorial to the Buddhist faith. The monument, six and one-half feet tall, is divided into panels, each devoted to a particular aspect of the life and teachings of Buddha. Such a Buddhist stone was a form of votive offering, typically commissioned by a large number of donors whose names were carved on the base and back of the object.

Daoism, and advocated the abolition of Daoist temples and the return of Daoist priests to the laity. He banned wine and meat at the imperial table and forbade the use of living things for medicinal purposes or as sacrificial objects.

Wu sponsored the construction of Buddhist temples—one of them, built in memory of his father, large enough to house 1,000 monks. He convened religious assemblies where prominent monks—and sometimes the emperor himself—delivered lectures on a particular sutra of the Buddhist scriptures. To raise funds for the monks he occasionally gave himself up to a temple as a menial and then had his courtiers pay huge amounts of treasure for his release.

So immersed in Buddhism was Wu, in fact, that in the late years of his reign he slighted state matters. Corruption blighted his court, where the aristocrats set a tone of decadent privilege. One witness noted: "There was not one of them who did not perfume his garments, shave his face, use powder and rouge, ride in a carriage with long awnings, wear elevated clogs, sit on square cushions, . . . lean on soft silk bolsters arranged with curios or trinkets on each side." Finally, civil war broke out.

In 549, when his enemies besieged Jiankang, Wu sent a kite aloft to inform allies outside the city of his plight. The ploy, which resulted in the earliest written reference to what was apparently a Chinese invention—the kite—failed to save the city or Emperor Wu, who was imprisoned and left to starve in his palace.

In addition to civil wars, armed conflict between the forces of north and south was endemic during the long separation of the two Chinas. Usually it was a matter of southern armies trying to recapture the north from the aliens and thus restore the empire. In 347, the south had reconquered what would later be the province of Sichuan. And briefly in 529, Emperor Wu's top general had held the northern capital, Luoyang. But southern armies failed repeatedly to hold substantial territories north of the Yangtze, despite the fact that for long periods the north was more unstable than the south. In the north, a confusion of alien dynasties sometimes ruled simultaneously, so that the region split into many kingdoms. It was no wonder then that Chinese historians labeled this era the Sixteen Kingdoms of the Five Barbarians.

The first alien regime in the north, that of the Xiongnu, or Huns, who had triggered the north-south split in 317, soon fell to tribal turmoil. Hun leaders who tried to rule on the Chinese model, with a bureaucratic centralized government, were overthrown by the Hun general Shi Le. Shi hated the Chinese and reverted to tribal rule. He terrorized the Chinese, subjecting many to serflike conditions or slavery.

Memories of his reign smoldered. In 349, sixteen years after Shi Le's death, Chinese rebels, in an unprecedented explosion of racial hatred, massacred his successors and an estimated 200,000 Huns. Another people of Mongolian background, the Xianbei, seized the throne. Meanwhile, other kingdoms were being carved out of the north, including one founded in western Gansu by a native Chinese general.

In the subsequent strife and confusion of the Sixteen Kingdoms, one barbarian leader stood out. He was the Chinese-educated Tibetan general Fu Jian, who in 357 began his rule of the north's central provinces. A superb organizer, Fu Jian brought together his own Tibetans, native Chinese, and remnants of the Huns and other tribes in an army that was military rather than tribal in structure. He also broke with tribal tradition by creating an infantry—an idea that was anathematic to the Mongolian nomads, who always fought mounted, but made sense to the Tibetans, old sheepherders used to traveling on foot. His infantry, composed largely of Chinese conscripts, proved particularly effective in laying siege to fortified towns.

Eyes closed in meditation, a bodhisattva prays to Buddha. According to Buddhist doctrine, bodhisattvas were wise and compassionate disciples of Buddha who had purposely foregone their ascension to Nirvana—in order to devote their lives to the spiritual well-being of humanity. The bodhisattva's elegant garb and jewelry indicate his earthly status.

Fu Jian's army subdued one neighboring kingdom after another. By 376, he ruled all of northern China, occupying both ancient capitals, Luoyang and Changan, and controlling the western trade routes. But it was not enough. Like Liu Yuan, the ambitious Hun leader who had deposed the Chinese rulers of the north, Fu Jian envisioned restoring the entire Han empire—with himself at its helm.

In 383, he marched south. His army, by some accounts, numbered nearly one million men—far more than the Eastern Jin rulers could muster. But his horsemen, used to the mountainous north, weakened in the unaccustomed heat, and his expedition bogged down on the soggy plains along the Yangtze. Schedules went awry, and supplies failed to arrive on time. To make matters worse, the outmanned southerners attacked isolated units before they could maneuver into larger formation and bribed some units to defect. They also spread false reports about their numbers that panicked much of the northern army. At the Battle of Fei River in Anhui province, the northerners were defeated as much by such psychological warfare as by force.

Fu Jian beat a hasty retreat. At this sign of his vincibility, northern enemies took up arms. Within a year, the north fragmented once again, into five splinter kingdoms. Fu Jian himself fell in an assassination arranged by a turncoat Tibetan follower.

A beneficiary of the turmoil in the north was Buddhism. Monasteries with walls strong enough to withstand attack became havens against the destruction. Merchants used the monks as bankers and sometimes warehoused their goods and secluded themselves and their families within the walls. Others seeking to evade taxes or labor conscription also took refuge there. Buddhism, in fact, provided a common meeting ground for Chinese and barbarian alike during an era of uncertainty.

The faith was promoted by many northern rulers. Foreigners themselves, they had no reason to mistrust Buddhism as an alien religion. Whereas in the south Buddhism took root because of the aristocracy's interest in its philosophical aspects, northerners gravitated to Buddhist monks famed as soothsayers or as practitioners of magic: The first monk to gain everyday entrée to a northern court was a Central Asian named Fuotudeng who, to the astonishment of the Hun emperor, could make lotus flowers materialize in a vase that appeared to contain only water.

Alien chieftains made their most significant contribution to Buddhism in sponsoring the translation of scriptures. In 382, near the end of the reign of the Tibetan Fu Jian, one of his army expeditions ventured into Kucha in Central Asia and captured an eminent monk named Kumarajiva. The monk was the son of an Indian father and a Kuchan princess and had been dedicated to the church at the age of seven. Now in his early thirties, he was known for his sense of humor, his failure to be celibate, and his skill in translating languages, among them Sanskrit and Chinese.

Kumarajiva was taken to China, where power politics kept him in captivity for nearly twenty years. Then, in 402, the current Tibetan sovereign in the old capital of Changan installed him there as the director of a group of scholars. Kumarajiva and his colleagues translated no fewer than ninety-eight lengthy Buddhist scriptures from the Sanskrit. Describing the difficulty in preserving the qualities of the original text, Kumarajiva once said: "Translating Sanskrit into Chinese is like feeding a man with rice chewed by another; it is not merely tasteless, it is nauseating as well." The original Indian versions would be lost in ensuing centuries, but fifty-two of Kumarajiva's translations would survive to remain in the Buddhist canon in modern times.

Many of the texts for such translations were carried home from India by Chinese monks who made the arduous pilgrimage west to Buddhist holy places. The trek

Monumental figures carved from solid limestone stand guard over the temple of Feng-xian Si at Longmen, a Buddhist shrine on the Yi River, ten miles from the southern capital of Luoyang. At center, Tuo-wen Tian, Guardian of the North, is flanked by a bodhisattva *(left)* and a muscular *li shi,* or strong man *(right).*

across Central Asia required climbing mountains, negotiating countless rivers, and crossing deserts on trails beset by bandits and warring hordes. Despite the difficulties, sixty-one Chinese pilgrims visited the Indian holy places during the fifth century.

A contemporary of Kumarajiva, Faxian, made the journey in 399, when he was more than sixty years of age. After a 259-day march to India, he decided to return by ship, via Ceylon and Java. But a storm carried his vessel hundreds of miles off course, and he spent almost a year at sea. He somehow preserved the manuscripts he had laboriously copied. Faxian's account of his adventures, together with the writings of other pilgrims, were to prove invaluable to future historians, since they helped establish a chronology for events in India, where people rarely recorded dates.

Meanwhile, in 386, soon after the collapse of the empire of the Tibetan Fu Jian, a new kingdom that would prove capable of uniting the fractious north was established in upper Shansi province, just south of the Great Wall. This dynasty, which was to be known as the Northern Wei, was founded by the Tuoba people, nomads who had moved into the border region from southeastern Mongolia during the third century. Badly in need of new sources of food, the Tuoba had expanded eastward into the fertile plains at the expense of neighboring kingdoms. While gaining new agricultural ground, they also improved the agricultural economy in the region around their capital in northern Shansi, Pingcheng (later called Datong), by deporting almost half a million farm workers there from the newly conquered eastern territories.

During the early decades of the fifth century, the Wei expanded their territory westward, conquering kingdoms one by one. By 440, they had unified northern China, ending the period of the Sixteen Kingdoms of the Five Barbarians. A decade later, their armies pushed down as far as the Yangtze River, annexing bits of southern territory, but the Wei proved unable or unwilling to reunite the entire empire.

The Tuoba and other barbarian conquerors left a cultural imprint on the northern Chinese. From the nomads came the large hat affected by males of the Chinese aristocracy—ornamented by sable tails and pheasant feathers. To keep up with fast-riding nomads, Chinese cavalry abandoned their loose upper garment, long skirt, and low shoes and adopted the intruders' belted tunic, trousers, and boots. The Chinese also adopted the stirrup used by riders from the steppes; now, like the nomads, their mounted archers could stand to shoot, their feet securely anchored.

But the effect of the Chinese on their alien conquerors ran far deeper, ranging from the dynastic names the invaders adopted to the ways in which they ruled. In selecting the name *Wei* for their dynasty, the Tuoba followed other barbarian kingdoms in borrowing honored imperial names from Chinese history. And from the beginning, the Wei government relied on members of the Chinese aristocracy as advisers. As more and more farmland with its sedentary peasant population was incorporated into the empire, a Chinese-style bureaucracy grew up to administer these new holdings.

Much of this happened without any real plan, but beginning with Emperor Xiaowen, who took the throne in 471, the Wei embarked upon a policy of sinicization. Xiaowen made Chinese the official language of the court and decreed that Tuoba nobles adopt Chinese dress and customs and trade their polysyllabic clan names for orthodox Chinese surnames. He also encouraged intermarriage among the leading families of the Tuoba and Chinese. To increase respect for Tuoba aristocrats descended from illiterate cattle breeders and raiders living in tents, the emperor issued a decree that put them on equal social footing with the leading Chinese.

Xiaowen's most dramatic step toward sinicization was transplanting the Wei capital 600 miles south from the northern border region into the ancient Chinese heartland. He rebuilt the old capital Luoyang, which had been abandoned after the Huns sacked it in 311, and transferred the court there in the years 493 and 494. Relocating the capital in Luoyang also promoted the growth of Buddhism. For much of the Wei dynasty, it was the favored faith. One emperor, Tuoba Hung, became so fascinated by Buddhism that he abdicated in 471 to devote himself to studying the religion. Unlike the south, where monks doggedly clung to their independence, the Wei state succeeded in making Buddhism virtually the official religion. The emperor appointed a supreme prelate—officially, chief of the Office to Illumine the Mysteries—to oversee the northern establishment. The first of these monks justified bowing down to imperial authority by asserting that the emperor was a reincarnation of the Buddha.

The exception to the glowing record of religious and state relations under the Wei occurred during the 440s, when a leading Daoist gained the emperor's ear and began to criticize the Buddhists. The monasteries were growing wealthy at state expense, he alleged. By casting all those bells and statues, they were causing a metal shortage. In addition, many monks were a threat or an embarrassment, sparking peasant rebellions in the provinces or even publicly immolating themselves—supposedly "for the salvation of all living creatures." The Daoist criticisms were familiar and had some legitimacy. The emperor responded by persecuting Buddhists and executing monks.

With the move to Luoyang a half century later, however, the Buddhists won ample recompense. The capital became the center of Buddhism in East Asia. Men and women were converted in record numbers, contributing to the estimated two million who entered the priesthood during the reign of the Northern Wei. One observer counted no fewer than 1,367 monasteries in Luoyang. Temples occupied nearly a third of the city, an imperial prince complained, spilling over into the meat and wine markets so that "Sanskrit chants and the cries of butchers unite their echoes under contiguous eaves" and temples "are wrapped in the odors of meat."

Criminals and their families served in many of the monasteries here and elsewhere in the north. They were slaves of the state who were assigned to the temples to cut wood, cultivate the fields, and perform other manual labor. Temple slavery proved to be so economically productive that it soon spread to the Buddhist church in other Asian countries. Many of the slaves became converts to Buddhism.

One of the largest temples in Luoyang, the Jingming, sprawled like a palace among hills and ponds and contained more than 1,000 cells. Here, once a year, all the city's statues of the Buddha were assembled to launch the parade celebrating the Buddha's birthday. Amid music, chanting, and scattered flowers, the procession wound its way through streets lined with the faithful to the gates of the imperial palace. This annual procession, with its bobbing ranks of big and little Buddhas, testified to the religious fervor sweeping China. Testimony on a more monumental scale could be found in the magnificent cave sculptures that were carved out of northern cliffs during the Wei era. Like the cathedrals of European Christianity, these works provided enduring symbols of the faith's power to transform people and their art and landscape.

The first major sculptures, depicting scenes from the scriptures and images of Buddha up to 160 feet tall, were chiseled from the steep river cliffs at Yungang, just west of the first Wei capital at Pingcheng. The work, which began in 489, was probably inspired by rock sanctuaries visited by Chinese pilgrims in India and Central Asia. The Buddhist monks got the emperor to pay for all of it. After the transfer of the capital to Luoyang, new cave sculptures were begun just to the south of that city, at

Longmen. Here, as at Yungang, generations of sculptors labored for at least three centuries. They cut so many images of the Buddha from the Longmen rock that no subsequent census was able to arrive at an accurate count: one twentieth-century enumeration totaled 97,306; another reached 142,289.

A prime beneficiary of the Northern Wei's ascendancy, Buddhism also played a role in its decline. In 515, the widow of a newly deceased emperor seized power in the name of her son, who was still a child. Empress Dowager Ling was an extraordinary woman, an athlete possessed of steel nerves and an unerring aim that enabled her to outshoot all her male courtiers with the bow and arrow. She was both a devout Buddhist and a generous spender; when her father died, she gave a vegetarian banquet for 10,000 monks. Among other extravagances, Ling ordered the construction of the Yongning Temple, Luoyang's most opulent monastery and the tallest structure in all of China. The temple featured a tower adorned with bells of gold and soaring so high that its gleaming silhouette could be glimpsed from thirty miles away.

Building the temple practically exhausted the imperial treasury, undermining Ling's power, which already had proved fragile. Her land seethed with a civil war touched off in the northern frontier region in 523 by Tuoba and other non-Chinese soldiers. These warriors had kept their tribal ways and deeply resented the court's wholesale changeover to Chinese customs and the extravagance prevalent in Luoyang, where, it was said, merchants had become so wealthy and sinicized that even their servants dressed in gold and silver brocades.

The tragic finale came in 528. Empress Dowager Ling, fearing that her son the emperor was becoming too independent, killed him and enthroned a younger son. Luoyang blazed with revolt and confusion. A Tuoba general led a coup during which Ling and the new infant emperor were drowned in the Yellow River and 2,000 of her courtiers were murdered. Six years later, the Yongning Temple was destroyed by fire. During that same year of 534, the Northern Wei dynasty ended after roughly a century in power. The north split into rival states—Eastern Wei and Western Wei—each claiming the old Tuoba heritage as well as the Wei name.

But the north would not remain long divided, nor indeed would all of China. Although sharp regional differences persisted, the people everywhere had much in common. All shared the same written language; a poem or an imperial decree inscribed in one part of the vast land could be read and understood more than a thousand miles away. Through acculturation and intermarriage, the barbarians of the north and the aboriginal people of the south were becoming indistinguishable from the original ethnic Chinese. And Buddhism crossed boundaries of geography and class, becoming the religion of the masses and the upper classes, north and south.

All that was lacking was a sufficiently powerful leader and army to weld together the millions of people residing within the borders of the old Han empire. That was remedied late in the sixth century. In 577, the heirs of the Western Wei conquered their rival, the Eastern Wei. Four years later, Yang Jian, a general of combined Chinese and barbarian Xianbei ancestry who had been born in a Buddhist temple, usurped the throne and proclaimed the new Sui dynasty. In 589, his Sui army marched south to Jiankang and easily subdued the last and weakest of the southern dynasties, reunifying all of China and ending—for a time—the upheaval and strife.

Then, fittingly, this emperor of mixed blood launched a highly visible campaign to identify himself with Buddhism, relying on the popularity of a religion once considered alien to help heal old wounds and consolidate his new empire.

A CHRONICLE IN CLAY

Not every culture that left an important legacy recorded its history in writing. During the first millennium AD, the rugged strip of land between the Pacific Ocean and the Andes (present-day Peru) was home to several complex societies that made their marks without the benefit of a written language. Instead, these peoples preserved their myths and mores in compelling images—scratched on the desert floor, painted on the walls of temples, woven into fabrics, or modeled in clay scooped from the banks of ponds. The clay sculptures, with their expressive features and realistic details, would prove especially revealing to those who later sought to understand the ways of these early Americans. In the case of the Moche, a versatile and sometimes violent people who dominated the river valleys of northern Peru through the seventh century, the surviving clay images afford dazzling glimpses into the heart of the culture.

Moche artists portrayed an array of vivid characters—ranging from deities to drunkards—on functional clay containers, many of them equipped with stirrup-shaped spouts. Such spouts in fact made pouring difficult, indicating that the vessels were prized more for their ingenious forms than for any practical purpose. The majority of these containers were fashioned in a pair of baked-clay half-molds cast from a solid model of the particular figure under study—a fisherman paddling his reed boat, perhaps, or the bust of some solemn dignitary (above). The reusable half-molds were lined with layers of wet clay. Once the clay was firm enough, the molds were removed

and the two clay pieces were joined. The stirrup spout itself and ornaments such as the fisherman's paddle were modeled separately and attached to the pot, which was subsequently painted and fired.

Whatever earthly use these decorative vessels served, most eventually ended up in a grave or tomb. One Moche lord was buried with seventy-five of them. That such works were associated with the afterlife is not difficult to understand, since many of them portrayed supernatural beings or humans in the act of appeasing gods. One of the chief Moche deities was represented in clay with a human face, but with the fangs of a cat—a reflection of the jaguar cult that had held people in thrall from Peru to Mexico for more than a thousand years. Like the dreaded jaguar, the fanged god was ever in need of fresh victims, and it was the duty of Moche lords and warriors to ply him with offerings of human blood. Once such fierce spirits were satisfied, however, they were prepared to shower the earth with blessings, providing humans with the herbs necessary to cure the sick and the bounties of sea and soil needed to feed the hungry.

Clay portraits of the Moche making use of such heaven-sent gifts reveal customs that would prevail in remote areas of Peru into modern times. Then as now, men wielding clubs stalked sea lions along the fog-shrouded coast, weary farmers sought a lift by chewing coca leaves or drinking maize beer, and healers invoked the sacred spirit of the owl as they peered into the darkness of the sick man's soul to spot the source of his malady.

A Moche lord sits with a striped cat at his side on this throne-shaped vessel equipped with the characteristic stirrup spout. The lord's earspools and conical headdress—similar to that worn by the fanged god on the opposite page—denote his lofty status, while the presence of the cat, the chief emblem of supernatural power among the Moches, suggests that this regal figure is in touch with the gods.

Another lord perches on a throne decorated at the base with two jaguarlike creatures face-to-face. The Moche inherited elements of the jaguar cult from the Chavín, who dominated the Andean region in the first millennium BC.

This Moche work portrays the fanged god—with a cat totem on his headdress—staring into space, backed by awe-struck mortals huddled below Andean peaks. The figure draped over the central peak appears to have been sacrificed. Other Moche vessels show humans with their fingers clenched in a shape simulating the five peaks portrayed here—a gesture probably meant to invoke the powers of the mountain-dwelling spirits.

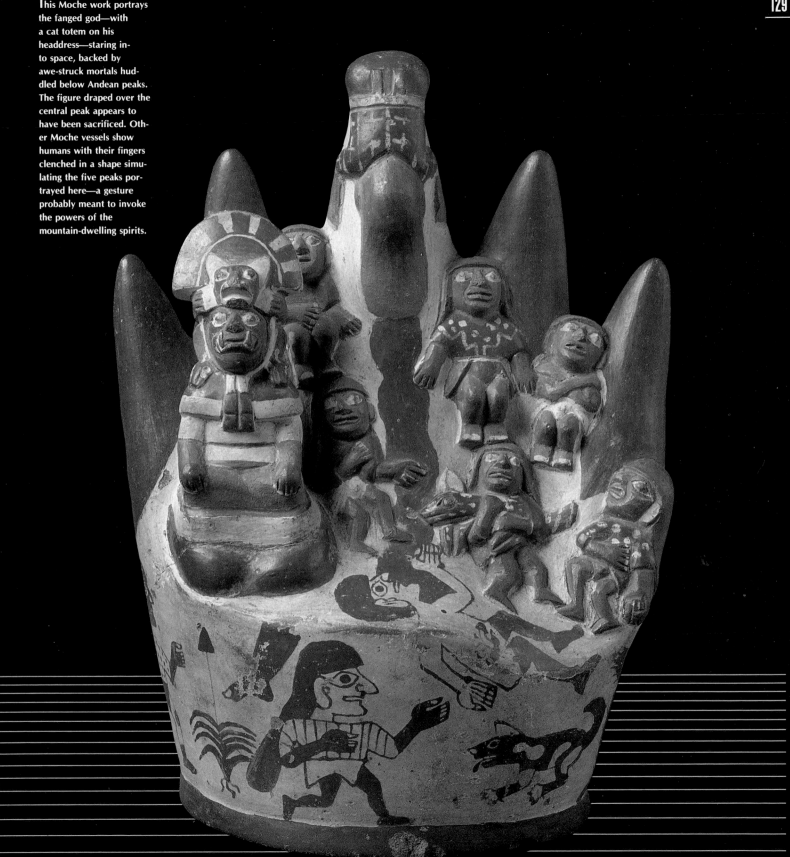

A decapitated victim lies at the feet of the fanged god, who holds the broad *tumi* knife used to carry out the sacrifice; a cat's head crowns the god, while at the base of the vessel painted felines spread their jaws menacingly. In real-life bloodlettings, the tumi would be wielded by a priest or lord, who might appear masked as a god.

An owl-headed healer—either a supernatural being or a human masked as one—draws medicine from a mortar atop this vessel. The painted objects on strings below the mortar are dried *espingo* seeds, used through the centuries in the region to treat stomachaches, hemorrhages, and other disorders. Like the jaguar god, the Moche owl spirit had its predatory side—it was sometimes portrayed with a tumi in one hand and a severed head in the other. But once appeased, the owl spirit would freely endow human healers with its wisdom and vision.

Above, a healer ministers to a patient, who lies naked except for a cap. Healers called to treat powerful figures in the society might be slain if the patient succumbed.

Below, two kneeling Moche warriors wield the principal weapon of the region—a mace with a conical head. The warrior at left also grips a small shield for fending off blows. Such fighting men received further protection from helmets with ear shields and quilted-cotton body armor, which was thick enough to halt darts shot by foes. While the Moche were known to embark on campaigns against their neighbors, they feuded internally too. Among the fruits of war were prisoners, who could be sacrificed to the gods.

bove, a princely Moche warrior with large ear-spools and a square shield brings his mace down on the head of a victim. A ceremonial headdress, with its cresent-shaped crest, appears in relief below his shield. The object resembling a sacrificial tumi knife, dangling from the victim's waist, is in fact part of his costume—a symbolic reminder, perhaps, of the fate awaiting the vanquished.

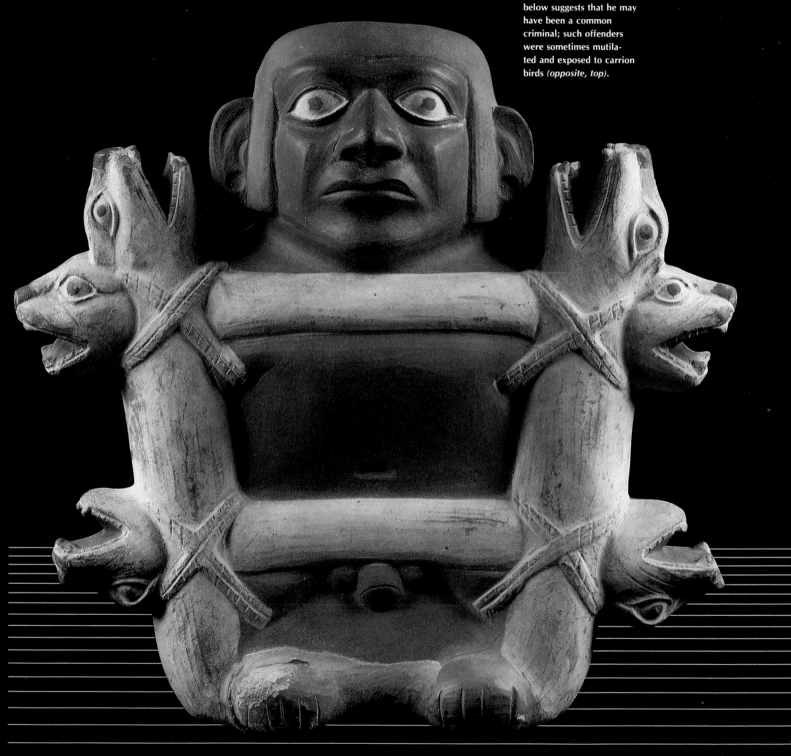

A captive stands tied to a rack made of wooden stakes carved with cat heads. In Moche art, prisoners of war were usually portrayed with ropes around their necks, awaiting ritual sacrifice (opposite, bottom). The absence of a collar on the victim below suggests that he may have been a common criminal; such offenders were sometimes mutilated and exposed to carrion birds (opposite, top).

A feline representing the spirit to whom this prisoner's blood will be dedicated casts greedy eyes on the victim's neck. Not every warrior taken in battle was stripped of all dignity: Captured lords were carried in litters to the place of their sacrifice.

A bird pecks at the eye socket of a man whose lips and nose have apparently been sliced off by executioners. Among the Chimu, who dominated the region beginning around 900 and preserved many Moche customs, such a punishment was for theft, an offense against the gods.

A musician beating a drum sports a colorful costume of the sort Moche women crafted through weaving, embroidery, and appliqué; the flowing headdress, commonplace in this arid region, offered some protection against sun and swirling sand. Like the weavers' patterns, the music-makers' instruments were many and varied—including conch-shell trumpets, flutes, panpipes, rattles, ocarinas, and ceramic whistles and bugles.

One worker pours while another stirs in a timeless procedure that yields chicha, or maize beer. Moche artists left a record in clay not only of how their food and drink were prepared but of the sundry ingredients—including ears of maize and warty squashes.

A Moche fisherman plies his craft: a slender boat constructed of tule—a local reed—and propelled by means of a cane paddle. Other Moche portraits reveal that fishermen knelt atop such boats or sat astride them, but here the inspired artist has portrayed the craft as if it were an extension of the figure's body.

A midwife coaxes an infant from the womb as a helper grasps the waist of the mother, whose grimace tells of her triumphant anguish. The joy of birth among the Moche was followed all too often by sorrow as diseases took their toll of the young. Infants were honored at death no less than their elders, and their funeral goods included finely crafted clay toys.

A skeletal figure with animate eyes taps a drum as if to set the beat for a dance of the dead. Death figures were in fact portrayed in Moche paintings moving in line to the music of pipes and drums, suggesting that the deceased might somehow live on—like the clay images that accompanied them to the grave—to weave their haunting spell through the ages.

A VIGOROUS NEW WORLD

Even as the old imperial powers of Europe and Asia slid into decline, a new sense of energy and purpose seemed to infuse life in the Americas. From the highlands of Mexico to the sweltering jungles of Guatemala, in the Andes Mountains and coastal deserts of Peru, the quickening was evident. Among the cacti and the mahogany trees, great cities rose, centered on soaring stone pyramids and broad ceremonial squares. Trade among distant peoples flourished, populations expanded, and the arts and sciences reached triumphant new heights. American sculptors carved images of astonishing complexity. American weavers fashioned textiles as fine as any in the world. Astronomers plotted the arcs of the planets with uncanny precision, and scribes set down dynastic chronologies according to a calendar so sophisticated no other civilization could match it.

Some parts of the Americas already had accomplished much. In the Peruvian Andes and along the Pacific coast below them, Chavín civilization—the earliest culture in America to warrant being termed a true civilization—had flourished for many centuries. It was a world of large ceremonial centers with fountains and pyramids, of verdant farmlands watered by extensive irrigation systems, of busy trade networks shifting foodstuffs and luxuries across a vast and geographically heterogeneous region. Although the Chavín world, for unknown reasons, began to crumble sometime after 400 BC, peoples who later lived in that part of South America preserved much Chavín culture.

To the north, in Mesoamerica, the region that stretches from around the Valley of Mexico south into Honduras, a people whom scholars later would call the Olmecs had spread their influence over a similarly large territory. For nearly a thousand years, Olmec traders and emissaries from the sultry lowlands of Mexico's Gulf Coast had threaded through the jungles and sierras, distributing their wares and culture. Their urban ceremonial complexes, with temples set on massive earthen platforms that flanked spacious plazas, were scattered over a thousand-mile-long stretch of Mesoamerica. The mysterious shadow of the central Olmec deity—half human, half jaguar—stalked both jungle and highland, its eerie visage glowering from sculpture and pottery. Around 400 BC the Olmec civilization, too, had begun to decay, and by AD 200 its great ceremonial centers had long since reverted to jungle. But memories of its gods and customs continued to resonate in subsequent societies in the region.

One place where the Olmec heritage survived with particular vigor was a hill later called Monte Albán, near where the city of Oaxaca, Mexico, would rise one day. Here, as early as 500 BC, the Zapotec people began erecting ceremonial monuments that closely followed the old Olmec designs. Unlike the Olmecs of the Gulf Coast jungles, the Zapotecs faced their pyramidal structures with stone, and the Zapotec styles of sculpture and pottery were distinctly their own. But their cultural similarity to the Olmecs was marked: They ritually sacrificed human beings to their gods, as the Olmecs had; they were ruled by a powerful aristocracy with an impulse toward conquest; and they established trade with neighboring peoples.

The summit of Monte Albán stood some 1,300 feet above the surrounding countryside, an imposing declaration of the Zapotecs' dominance. They leveled the ground of the mountaintop, creating a smooth plateau about three-fifths of a mile wide. On this lofty pedestal the Zapotecs constructed an elaborate complex of terraces, courtyards, low stone pyramids, temples, and other ceremonial buildings, all laid out on a north-south axis. The job entailed a huge expenditure of human resources. Work crews numbering in the thousands—perhaps volunteers, but more likely workers whose labor was conscripted as a kind of tax—were needed to level the earth and to quarry and haul the stone. Tools, materials, and supplies, including food and water for the workers, had to be hauled up from the valley below, probably by porters: The Zapotecs had no beasts of burden, since there were no suitable animals in Mesoamerica to domesticate for the purpose. And they had no wheeled vehicles—indeed no American people used the wheel for transportation, although their children played with wheeled toys. These builders may have had pulleys, however, which would have eased construction jobs such as that on Monte Albán.

One of the first structures they built stood at one corner of the plateau on a masonry platform faced with sandstone slabs. The building was probably a temple, but its base also served as a monument to Zapotec military strength. Zapotec artists carved in low relief on the sandstone some 150 nude male figures that at first glance appear to be cavorting in odd, rubbery positions, as though performing some kind of crazy dance. Future archaeologists, in fact, would mistakenly call them "Danzantes." But the dance the sculptors were illustrating was one of death. The figures were corpses strewn about in the haphazard poses in which they fell. With closed eyes and gaping mouths and blood spewing from their loins in elaborate scrolls, they memorialized enemies who had been captured and sacrificed.

Terrible in war, the Zapotecs were also deeply intellectual. Their predecessors, the Olmecs, had developed a rudimentary form of pictographic script to use in recording dates in combination with the very complex and accurate Olmec calendar, which was based on precise and sophisticated astronomical observations. The Zapotecs went a step further, creating a hieroglyphic script that was the earliest known system of writing in the Americas, although it was probably used only to record names and events. Zapotec carvers inscribed in hieroglyphs the names of several of the Danzante figures on the sandstone tableau. In addition, on some of the slabs they carved bars and dots that probably represented numbers, perhaps dates. On another building, the stone carvers depicted scores of heads, each upside down, severed from its body, and accompanied by a hieroglyph marking the date and spelling out the name of a neighboring town. The significance was clear to viewers then and later: This was a record of the conquests by which the warriors from Monte Albán extended their domain across the surrounding territory. Thus the Zapotecs were the first Americans to record their history.

They also found time for athletic contests—at least for a ritual ball game similar to one the Olmecs had played, which was taken up by other peoples throughout Mesoamerica. At Monte Albán the Zapotecs constructed a special place for their game, a long sunken courtyard, roughly I-shaped, with sloping stone sides. The game

By the third century AD, several major cultures were flourishing in Mesoamerica. From Monte Albán, a city of imposing pyramids and plazas, the Zapotecs fanned out to subjugate scores of neighboring communities, bringing with them irrigation technology and recording their exploits in writing. In the Valley of Mexico to the northwest, the planned city of Teotihuacán with its vast temples and bustling workshops emerged as the hub of an enterprising society that dominated trade in the region. Farther south, the Maya wrought wonders in the rain forest of Petén, clearing the dense growth to lay the foundations for a number of cities, compiling historical annals based on elaborate calendars, and detailing their fierce rituals in eloquent images.

resembled a particularly fast and rugged variety of basketball. Two teams vied for possession of a hard rubber sphere about the size of a grapefruit, which they attempted to knock through a stone ring affixed to the side of the court. What made the contest especially challenging was that the players could not use their hands; they struck the ball instead with elbows, knees, or hips. A score, therefore, was hard to come by—so difficult that in a later Mexican era, a player who managed to propel the ball through the hoop was awarded the jewels and clothing of the spectators.

The game was dangerous. The solid ball sometimes traveled at such high speed that it could maim or even kill. Players protected themselves with heavy padding on elbows, knees, and hips, and a sturdy helmet with a barred visor. And although winners might earn glory and riches, losing could be very costly or downright hazardous, depending on the stakes. In some groups, the teams represented rival political factions, and the game's outcome determined weighty matters of state. In others, the losers became the slaves of the winners. So seriously did some pre-Columbian American peoples take the game that the vanquished captain was considered to have

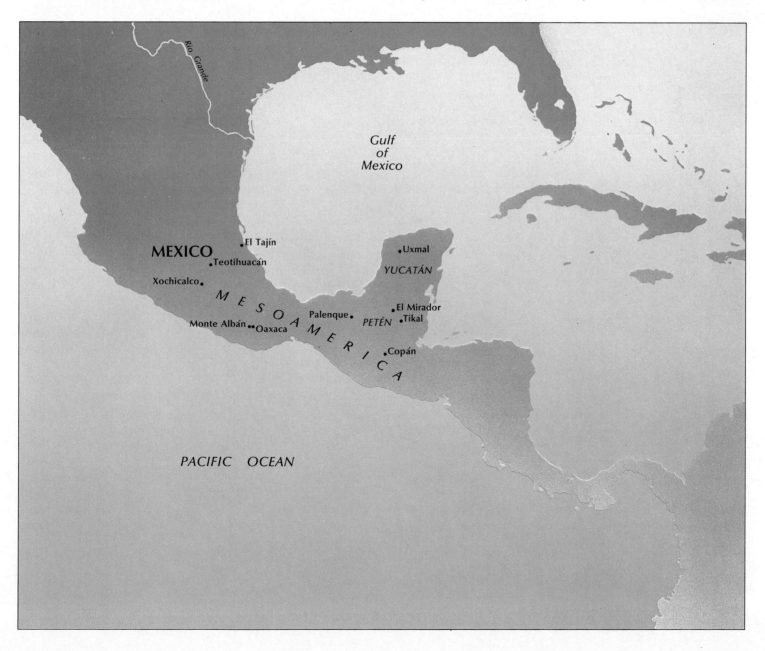

been ordained to carry a message to the gods—and would fulfill that assignment by giving up his life on the sacrificial altar. Clearly the game was more than mere sport. For both players and spectators, it was a sacred ritual, one that perhaps mimicked the movements of the stars and mirrored the uncertain fate of human beings on earth.

By the beginning of the second century AD, the Zapotecs had spread their power across the hills and valleys to embrace more than 200 surrounding communities. Their conquered neighbors received more than the opportunity to die in a Zapotec sacrificial rite; the victors also bestowed the economic benefits of sophisticated political organization. Extensive irrigation systems soon webbed the semiarid valley bottoms, increasing the yields of corn, beans, squash, and other staples. As agricultural productivity rose, so did the population. In time, Monte Albán grew into a bustling urban center of as many as 20,000 people, who lived in stone or earthen dwellings. Strategically placed atop its rocky bastion and protected from alien incursion by the mountain chains that encircled the region, the Zapotec capital would remain a stable, influential power in southern Mexico for hundreds of years to come.

While Zapotec civilization was still thriving, an even more robust expression of urban genius began to make itself felt several hundred miles to the northwest, in the mountain-rimmed fastness of the Valley of Mexico. This well-watered, 3,000-square-mile basin, situated roughly midway between the Atlantic and the Pacific and between the Rio Grande and the Yucatán Peninsula, was a setting of great promise. The land dropped down from a dry sagebrush plateau, which formed a kind of natural barrier on the north, to the valley's gentler terrain of prairie, marsh, and river bottom. A vast, shallow body of water, later called the Lake of the Moon by the Aztecs, teeming with fish and waterfowl, sprawled over much of the basin's floor; grasslands and scattered farm plots occupied the rest. To the south, a cluster of snowcapped volcanic peaks soared like guardian deities almost 18,000 feet into the tropic sky. Small game abounded; jackrabbit, turkey, quail, deer, wild dog all thrived in the bottomlands and among the pine and oak forests that sprouted across the lower mountain slopes. The valley was soon to become—and would remain, into the modern era—the center of civilization for all of Mexico. During the first century AD, early signs of that development were appearing in a small side pocket that extended northeast from the main valley. Here, on the plain of Teotihuacán, architects were laying out the street grid for what would rapidly become the largest, most aggressively cosmopolitan city in the Americas.

The valley's chief crop was corn. Because of the high elevation, nearly a mile above sea level, the climate tended to be more temperate than tropical. Spring rains induced the newly sown kernels to sprout; rainfall dwindled in summer when dry weather was needed for harvesting, then poured in earnest during the autumn months, soaking the soil for the next year's crop. Winters were clear, dry, and frosty. Conditions could be somewhat harsher in the Teotihuacán spur, with earlier cold snaps and occasional local droughts. But more than eighty freshwater springs dotted the plain, offering a dependable water supply.

Given the Valley of Mexico's natural advantages, it is surprising that urban civilization had not taken firm root here earlier. During a thousand years of Olmec hegemony in southern Mexico, the valley had remained a cultural backwater, its inhabitants content to tend their corn and live as primitive agricultural villagers. They were not entirely untouched by Olmec culture, however. A low, oval-shaped earthen mound of the type that marked Olmec ceremonial sites loomed above the plain at

Cuicuilco, a place that one day would be swallowed up by Mexico City. The builders of the mound had arrived some time around 300 BC, and they stayed on for several centuries, modeling ceramic figurines in Olmec style and perhaps sending missionaries and traders into the surrounding farmlands. Their efforts undoubtedly had a civilizing effect. But Cuicuilco itself was abandoned, and sometime after the first century an outpouring of lava from a nearby volcano buried the remains of its ceremonial mound.

One reason for Cuicuilco's decline may have been the rapid ascendance of Teotihuacán. Groups of settlers had farmed the Teotihuacán area for perhaps 400 years, living in small stone or adobe villages beside the springs or stream beds. But agricultural techniques were rudimentary. The basic farming system was slash-and-burn: A field was cleared, the brush set afire, and corn kernels planted in the ashes. A few years later, after the soil had lost its nutrients, the field would be allowed to lie fallow while the farmers moved on to slash and burn new acreage. Using these methods, perhaps 6,000 people supported themselves in reasonable comfort in the Teotihuacán area. Then suddenly, for reasons that are only partly understood, the population began growing rapidly.

Improvements in agriculture were surely one factor. At some point the people of Teotihuacán began terracing their fields and digging irrigation canals, thus ensuring a steadier flow of water. They also learned to develop marginal lands along the lagoons and stream beds. In one low-lying swampy sector they cut a grid of channels to drain off the water, thereby creating a series of rectangular, artificial islands that the Spanish later called chinampas. The Teotihuacanos raised the ground level of the islands with scoops of mud and pond weeds pulled from the surrounding water. The chinampas were wonderfully fertile, and they represented a giant stride forward from the old slash-and-burn days. The valley's inhabitants now grew more squash, pumpkins, tomatoes, various types of beans, plums, and avocados to supplement their basic diet of ground corn.

But the Teotihuacanos also discovered another avenue of development. In the hills behind the future city lay one of Mexico's finest deposits of obsidian, a hard, brittle volcanic glass that could be flaked to a razor-sharp edge. It was an ideal material for making tools and weapons. Several obsidian workshops were already in business by the end of the second century BC, and scores of others opened up in ensuing decades, turning out the knives, axheads, scrapers, dart points, and other implements that hastened the development of civilization. With firm control over the region's most valuable resource, Teotihuacán may have risen to glory because it was the primary manufacturing center of Mesoamerica.

Whatever it was that set them going, the Teotihuacanos began to build on a colossal scale. Most ancient American cities grew haphazardly, starting as small clusters of family dwellings, each with a ceremonial mound or pyramid at its center, which succeeding generations gradually embellished and enlarged. Not this one. Teotihuacán was planned from the start. Architects surveyed the ground and laid out a rectangular gridwork of streets and apartment blocks that would cover more than eight square miles—an area as large as that of early imperial Rome.

The city's main axis was an arrow-straight, four-mile-long boulevard known to later Americans as the Avenue of the Dead, although in its day it bustled with energetic life. Luxurious, palacelike dwellings for the city's elite lined either side, along with broad plazas, a large central marketplace, and a pair of enormous temple-pyramids.

PYRAMID OF THE MOON

For sheer monumental size, nothing approaching these last two structures had ever been seen in the Americas.

The Pyramid of the Sun, flanking the avenue to the east, angled starkly upward in a series of majestic tiers. Its base, a square measuring nearly 700 feet on a side, covered as much ground as Egypt's mighty Pyramid of Cheops, the largest edifice in the ancient world, apart from China's Great Wall. A series of grand stone staircases led from a plaza below the pyramid to a platform at the summit, where a small, thatch-roofed temple stood. More than a million cubic yards of rubble and sun-baked brick formed the structure's interior. The whole pyramid was surfaced with cut stone dressed in plaster and possibly painted red. Construction began soon after Teotihuacán was laid out and was completed within a century. The Pyramid of the Moon, erected some centuries later at the north end of the avenue, followed the same austere design on a slightly smaller scale.

Dozens of lesser monuments and shrines adorned the city, most of them also adjacent to the central avenue. One particularly imposing cluster occupied a vast courtyard, more than a third of a mile square, near where a grand east-west thoroughfare crossed the Avenue of the Dead at right angles, marking the city's geographic center. A row of sloping platforms fringed the courtyard, like sentry posts. Along either side were two large buildings that may have served as administrative offices or perhaps as part of a palace.

Given the courtyard's size and location, it most certainly played an important role in government. At the same time, it was also a religious site. Its centerpiece was a small, elegantly proportioned pyramid embellished with carvings of mythological creatures. Long rectangular panels sheathed each of the pyramid's six ascending tiers, and from them lunged ranks of dragon heads with feathery ruffs: symbols of the Plumed Serpent, a god that personified cosmic forces. Alternating with these were carvings of the oddly geometric visage of the rain god—who would be known to modern scholars only by his Aztec name, Tlaloc—with his goggle eyes, shelflike upper lip, and menacing, long protruding teeth. Seashells, swirling waves, and other tokens of watery fertility abounded. The entire facade was coated in plaster—as were most other structures in Teotihuacán—and painted in brilliant hues of gold, blue-green, and vermilion.

Unlike the Zapotecs, the builders of Teotihuacán carved no dates or name glyphs by which later observers might piece together their history. Aside from some mysterious signs that they painted on walls, none of their writing would survive. None of their descendants would know what language they spoke, or even what they called themselves. The very name with which posterity would speak of their city was an Aztec word, bequeathed more than a thousand years after the fact by the empire that would come to occupy the region in the fifteenth century.

Teotihuacán meant "Place of the Gods" in the Aztec tongue. The Aztecs—who knew Teotihuacán as an ancient, holy ruin—believed that the gods had built the city

The main thoroughfare of Teotihuacán (below), known as the Avenue of the Dead, was dominated by two great pyramids, one dedicated to the sun and the other to the moon. A maze of dwellings, workshops, and shrines surrounded these monuments. Toward the south end of the avenue stood the so-called Citadel, a sunken court-yard that may have been the site of the royal palace; within the same enclosure rose the temple of Quetzal-coatl, the plumed-serpent god who bequeathed to humanity the nourishing gift of maize. Other life-sustaining deities worshiped in Teotihuacán included the rain god Tlaloc, a stern, goggle-eyed creature por-trayed at far left atop the ornate lid of an incense burn-er; the face peering out from the center of the lid may represent one of the god's priests. No less important to the survival of the city was the flayed god, Xipe Totec, shown at near left wearing the skin of a sacrificial vic-tim; the god's high priests would wear such flayed skins in a ceremony performed early each spring to ensure that the earth would regain its fertility.

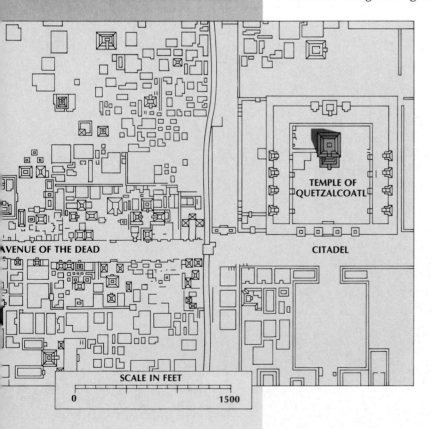

AVENUE OF THE DEAD

TEMPLE OF QUETZALCOATL

CITADEL

SCALE IN FEET

0   1500

and that its site had been the deities' birthplace. A universal cataclysm had obliterated both earth and heaven, said the tale, and so, on "the day that time began," the gods gathered there to set things right. An eternal fire blazed forth from the ground, and one after another the gods leaped into it. The first one emerged as the sun, the next as the moon, the third as an earth deity, and so on until time started ticking again, and the universe was restored to its proper form. This Aztec story explained their pantheon of deities, including Tlaloc and the Aztec version of a plumed serpent-god, Quetzalcoatl. But the story was not an Aztec invention. The line of belief stretched back unbroken to the heyday of Teotihuacán itself, when the city was the center of a cult of complex religious ideas that its missionaries—probably supported by armies—spread to the far corners of Mesoamerica.

Even the myth of the earth's generation found a resonant echo in the stones of Teotihuacán. Deep under the rubble core of the Pyramid of the Sun lay a set of volcanic caves, which Teotihuacanos even earlier than the pyramid builders had converted into a sanctuary for religious devotion. They gouged water channels into the rock floor and dug fire pits where they presented burnt offerings of lake fish and shells. The union of fire with water deep in the earth's recesses, the elements of creation brought together, would have been a reenactment of the primordial gesture of divine sacrifice.

The city's principal god was the deity of water and rain, Tlaloc. His image appeared everywhere. It was carved on the temple-pyramids and painted in the bright-colored murals on the walls of palatial residences. One particularly sprightly mural, the so-called Paradise of Tlaloc, showed the deity presiding over a luxuriant land of trees, flowers, birds, and butterflies. A host of naked figures danced among these tokens of nature's plenty, playing games, bathing in a river, angling for fish. Gleeful songs and hosannas, indicated by stylized scrolls in the painting, tumbled from the celebrants' lips. The figures may have represented the souls of the rain god's elect—perhaps victims of drowning, for example—who had been gathered up into a bountiful and joyous heaven.

Not all Teotihuacán's gods were as benevolent as Tlaloc. One who may have been

At left, a player in the ceremonial Mayan ball game—a contest in which the losers were often sacrificed—gestures like one whose life hangs in the balance. Slotted helmets such as the one portrayed here, which could be removed from this terra-cotta figure to reveal his features, shielded the contestant's head from the hard rubber ball as it flew about the court; a flat stone (foreground) may have been used to set the ball in motion, since touching it with the hands was forbidden. Those who played without helmets ran the risk of the contestant pictured at far right, who faces a hurtling ball of exaggerated dimensions. Like his opponents, this player wears a cumbersome yoke to protect his chest and waist, along with padding on knee, ankle, and hips. All three figures sport majestic headdresses, reflecting their high status; the scene may illustrate a fabled contest between gods and heroes.

present was an ominous deity known later to the Aztecs as Xipe Totec, the Flayed One, who represented the annual greening of the earth. To make sure springtime occurred on schedule, a senior priest would robe himself in a freshly stripped human skin in honor of Xipe Totec. And while the city's residents never went in for ritual slaughter on the massive scale of some neighboring cultures, they did regularly offer up the lives of selected fellow citizens to the gods, burying caches of bones from sacrificial victims in a number of local shrines.

The religious impulse that inspired Teotihuacán's great ceremonial buildings undoubtedly speeded its rise to prominence. As the center of a widely adopted faith, it was the holiest spot in Mexico. Pilgrims from distant parts joined thousands of Teotihuacanos crowding into the ceremonial plazas to watch the priests, all plumes and glitter, mount the steps of the pyramids to perform their rites.

By AD 400, Teotihuacán was nearing its zenith. Its population had reached 150,000 and was still rising. It was America's greatest urban complex, and one of the largest in the entire world. Its potentates had extended their rule over the full expanse of the Valley of Mexico and far beyond. A mass migration from countryside to city had brought in thousands of immigrants—either lured by jobs and religious awe or forcibly resettled to help build the monuments. Some 400 workshops were now busy manufacturing fine obsidian tools and weapons. In another 200 or more, potters turned out exquisite, multicolored ceramics, and other artisans made jewelry, carved masks, and fashioned religious figurines from jade, greenstone, and basalt inlaid with gems and shells. Some pottery was actually mass-produced in reusable molds that were refilled with wet clay again and again. Teotihuacano wares were in demand not only in the city and the nearby Valley of Mexico, but throughout Mesoamerica.

Although manufacturing was booming, the principal employer in Teotihuacán was most likely the state religious bureaucracy. Thousands of priests and acolytes spent their years paying homage at the shrines and attending to the details of ecclesiastical

In this enigmatic depiction of a Mayan court ceremony, an enthroned ruler wearing dark body paint looks down on a dwarf and a trio of kneeling attendants as musicians raise a salute with trumpets and a conch shell (far left). Such ceremonies were carried out in multi-chambered stone palaces, raised on terraces above the surrounding terrain and accommodating a royal family of up to 100 members, along with visiting lords and a retinue of servants, scribes, and artisans.

administration. Even greater numbers of workers toiled to build the holy structures. The city's rulers probably were selected from the priesthood, which may have been a hereditary group. A theocratic council of elders most likely drew up laws, shaped. state policies, marshaled work forces, and oversaw trade and agriculture. Priestly scribes kept the records of ritual and government, and temple astronomers maintained the calendar that dictated periods of planting and harvest. As the city's influence rolled out across Mesoamerica, officers of the state cult came to govern an increasing number of satellite towns and ceremonial sites.

The ruling classes lived in splendor in their palaces along the Avenue of the Dead. These buildings, all one-story structures, turned their backs to the street and faced inward. Stark masonry walls unrelieved by windows or other ornament formed their exteriors, while inside dozens of rooms with pillared fronts and ornamental entablatures gave out onto bright, airy courtyards. Roofs of earth-covered thatch shielded the rooms from sun and rain. The courts were paved and equipped with drains to carry off rainwater. Gleaming coats of plaster, polished to a high sheen, covered every surface, and many interiors were enlivened with vivid frescoes of gods and animals. The palaces were generally large, and each building probably housed several noble or priestly families along with their servants and retainers. One typical building contained forty-five rooms and seven courtyards; another, perhaps a barracks for lower-level priests, 300 rooms.

Common people lived farther from the main thoroughfares, in dwellings that were less elaborate and more crowded than the palaces along the Avenue of the Dead. These were large, one-story, rectangular tenement buildings, typically about sixty or seventy yards on a side, housing as many as 100 people in a warren of apartments reached by a maze of narrow corridors that twisted and meandered through the structure. Rooms varied in size from about twenty feet square down to closet dimensions. Some opened directly onto courtyards and small patios, but interior rooms in the same apartments were dark and probably depended for ventilation on some kind of openings in the thatched roofs. And residents deep inside the building were at high risk if the compound caught fire.

The Teotihuacanos built more than 2,200 of these compounds, right to the edge of the city. There were no single-family dwellings. Many of the compounds housed only people who worked at a particular craft, such as potters, and their families. Some contained workshops for the artisans as well as living quarters. Workers in the obsidian industry lived and labored in two large compound areas—one near the Pyramid of the Moon, the other behind the Temple of the Plumed Serpent.

As Teotihuacán gained in size and prestige, it attracted large numbers of foreigners, who tended to live in their own quarters of the city. So many Zapotecs moved into one precinct, beginning around AD 400, that it took on the look and atmosphere of Monte Albán. The residents continued to follow some of the customs of their homeland, fashioning pottery and utensils in Zapotec style, carving monument stones with Zapotec glyphs, and burying their dead in stone-lined tombs. (Native Teotihuacanos favored cremation.)

All Teotihuacanos, rich and poor, arose at dawn and went to bed as night fell. At first light, artisans mustered in their workshops, and farmers, many of whom lived in city tenements, began the long trek out to the countryside to tend their crops. Women might help in the fields, but most of their chores were domestic—caring for the children, shopping in the market, weaving fabric for garments from cotton or the

The headdresses worn by Mayan kings, lords, and warriors were among the most elaborate status symbols ever devised. Concocted of exotic items culled from around the region—including parrot and macaw feathers, jaguar pelts, seashells, and jade—they told of men who received reverent tribute from those who depended on their prowess. Indeed, the headdresses of commanding figures often bore the features of a god, from whose gaping mouth the mortal's face would emerge—as illustrated at left by the clay figure holding a shield. Such crowns reflected the Mayan conviction that on ceremonial occasions their leaders became one with the gods. The lord portrayed above, for example, is wearing an animal-skull mask so as to invoke the spirit of a sacrificial god before entering battle.

Perhaps it was with such ceremonies in mind that Mayan skulls were often purposely distorted. Shortly after birth, the soft cranium of many a noble Mayan was placed in a kind of vise—with one wooden clamp pressing against the forehead and the other against the back of the head. A youth treated in this fashion developed an elongated skull that must have been regarded as a sign of distinction—a prominence only accentuated when he came of age and donned his high headdress.

fibers of a pulpy-leafed plant called the maguey. Men wore a loincloth and perhaps a short kilt, women a long skirt and a short overblouse.

Residents of the compounds cooked their meals over pottery braziers. The women did the cooking, preparing corn tortillas, beans, squash, pumpkins, prickly-pear cactus, avocados, augmented by fish from the Lake of the Moon, or perhaps some wild game, such as birds downed by clay pellets projected from blowguns. The elite sometimes dined on turkey or roast dog—the only two animals domesticated in Mesoamerica. On feast days the meal might be washed down with pulque, a potent brew fermented from the maguey plant.

Feast days were not rare. Everyday business was relieved at frequent intervals by the excitement of religious festivals. There were rites of planting and rites of harvest, rituals to bring rain and to ensure that the sun marched across the heavens. And while some of these ceremonies entailed the sacrifice of human life, for most citizens they were a time of joyous abandon and a cornucopia of sight and sound. There would be dancing and singing and dressing up, much beating of drums and blowing of conch shells, and processions of priests in flamboyant plumed headgear weaving up and down the staircases of the great pyramids.

Teotihuacán was also the seat of an empire, and many of the city's people were involved in one way or another with expanding and maintaining that domain, if only by producing the trade goods that were shipped out to colonies. A degree of armed coercion must have been employed in bringing so many other peoples into their imperial sphere: It seems likely that Teotihuacán fielded a strong army of the spearmen who were depicted in some of their murals. The main vehicle of conquest, however, may well have been regiments of missionary priests, supported by battalions of traveling merchants bearing the wares of Teotihuacano artisans.

The leading exports were items made of obsidian. Obsidian tools from the city's workshops found their way into northern Mexico, east into the Yucatán, and as far south as the highlands of Guatemala. But Teotihuacano ceramics, too, were shipped out in large quantity—cylindrical jars with tripod bases, incense burners, pitchers, vases bearing the face of Tlaloc or worked to resemble dogs or other creatures. In return, the merchants would bring back jade from Guatemala, turquoise and greenstone from western Mexico, ornamental shells from both the Pacific and Gulf coasts, and cacao beans from the lowland jungles, probably used both for brewing chocolate and as a medium of exchange. Much of the regalia worn by the priests, such as jaguar skins and the iridescent green feathers of the quetzal bird, could be obtained only from the tropical jungles.

Besides peddling the city's own products, the imperial traders seem to have conducted much commerce between other widely scattered points. One thriving community just east of the Valley of Mexico was Cholula, whose ceremonial hub contained some seventy monuments and temples. Its central pyramid, a gigantic, adobe brick mound, became the largest artificial object in the Americas when it was completed around AD 700, surpassing in size Teotihuacán's Pyramid of the Sun and even Egypt's Pyramid of Cheops. The people of the Cholula area produced a fine ceramic ware, eggshell-thin and orange in hue, which Teotihuacán merchants distributed throughout Mesoamerica.

Wherever Teotihuacán's traders penetrated, they left their city's cultural imprint on local art and religion. The architects at Monte Albán began to construct tiered pyramids adorned with rectangular panels—much like the ones on Teotihuacán's

Temple of the Plumed Serpent and scores of other imperial monuments. So did builders at Cholula and in the southern city of Xochicalco and on the Gulf coast where Vera Cruz would be built one day. At the same time, Teotihuacán's religion spread out across Mesoamerica, its deities mingling with local gods. Most of these scattered cultures retained much of their independence even though they were allied to Teotihuacán. And for all their selective mimicry of the imperial style, most preserved their ancestors' ritual traditions.

With trade and religion as their most potent weapons, the Teotihuacanos established a number of satellite centers in far distant regions. Matacapán in the Tuxtla Mountains overlooking the Gulf coast probably functioned as a way station for caravans. Six hundred and fifty miles to the southeast of Teotihuacán, near an obsidian source in the Guatemala highlands, people residing in the city of Kaminaljuyú allied themselves with Teotihuacán. Either they or Teotihuacano traders who settled among them transformed the place into a miniature replica of Teotihuacán itself, building temples in the imperial style and living much the way people did in the city far to the north. What is most remarkable about these southern colonies is that they could exist at all—for the entire region was already controlled by another strong culture that itself was enjoying an exuberant expansion of prosperity and dominion.

The jungle kingdoms of the Maya were every bit as ancient as Teotihuacán, and their people just as enterprising. And while no single Mayan city would achieve the preeminence of the great northern metropolis, the Maya as a whole would create a civilization of even greater brilliance and refinement.

The Maya were different from other Mesoamerican people. They spoke a distinctive language. Their unique profiles—slanting forehead, beaklike nose, and full lips —would identify their descendants in Mexico and Guatemala throughout future ages. Yet like all people of this region, they owed a debt to the Olmecs. The Maya played the ritual ball game, built pyramids to elevate their temples, and engaged in rites of human sacrifice. They held jaguars in reverence—and their pantheon would come to include a host of deities, some of whose images were copied from Teotihuacán. The Maya took the already sophisticated Olmec calendar and rudimentary Olmec pictographic script and developed them to a new, high level of intellectual achievement. They were impeccable historians. The surface of every public building, of every stone marker in ceremonial plazas, was emblazoned with dates and genealogies, with accounts of battles and political alliances, with records of births, deaths, treaties, and ceremonies performed.

One of the oldest Mayan sites was Kaminaljuyú, the city that became a small replica of Teotihuacán. Possibly as early as 500 BC, a ceremonial complex of several hundred earthen mounds had been erected in Kaminaljuyú. Whatever the function of these structures, the site served partly as a burial ground. One departed Mayan lord was interred there in a log tomb with a trove of some 340 jade masks, jade ear ornaments, necklaces, stone bowls, and pottery vases of great beauty and grace. To help guide him into the world beyond, a number of the noble's retainers were sealed into the tomb with him.

But the crucible of Mayan culture was located in the lowland jungles, in particular the dense, steamy forest expanse in northern Guatemala known as the Petén, meaning "flat region" in Mayan. The Petén was a green, twilight domain of towering ceiba and mahogany trees; vines and moss draped their lower boughs, and toucans, ma-

caws, and howler monkeys darted through their upper branches. Deer, jaguar, and the racoonlike coati mundi lurked in the shadows of the forest floor, along with a venomous reptile, the barba amarilla, commonly known as the "two step": one step on the snake, the next in the grave. The thin forest soil, laid down on a limestone base, offered poor drainage and little nourishment for corn or other staple crops.

Nonetheless, by around 400 BC the Maya had cleared sections of forest to create farmlands. They cut drainage canals, built reservoirs, and soon were erecting tall masonry pyramids sheathed in native limestone. One of the earliest lifted above the jungle canopy at a place the Spanish later named El Mirador. A priest or nobleman emerging from the temple at its summit would have gazed across a plaza to dozens of surrounding buildings—lesser temples, monastic offices, dwellings for the tribal elite. Each one of them, like the pyramid itself, bore a coat of painted lime stucco and was embellished with various carvings or other artwork. The plaza was paved with a hard lime concrete.

El Mirador was clearly the work of a highly organized society. Mayan farmers there created and cultivated fields that were raised above the drainage waterways bordering them, much like the chinampas in the Valley of Mexico. Raised-field agriculture required sustained close cooperation among large numbers of farmers, possible only

Below, in a panoramic view of a Mayan vase painting, a lord with a goatee and an animal headdress appears twice with contrasting partners: a woman with dark hair and an acquiescent look *(far left)* and another with red hair and a fiercely determined expression. As this scene suggests, a Mayan dignitary might share his favors with more than one wife or courtesan, but women were not relegated to the background at court. Clad in wraps with bright batik designs and wearing flaring headdresses like that on the statuette at left *(inset)*, they rivaled their mates for splendor and figured prominently in ceremonies. And on several occasions, queens directed the affairs of Mayan city-states.

in well-organized groups. To build the urban center, cooperation was also necessary among master architects, sculptors, stone cutters, and mural painters—not to mention the regiments of laborers who did the hauling and lifting. Unlike Teotihuacán, El Mirador was not a truly heterogeneous city with a mix of high and low ranks. Only the elite lived in the central area. Laborers resided in outlying suburbs, and farmers, whose daily toil supported the economy, lived in the fields. Both of these working-class groups occupied pole-and-thatch houses with floors of plaster or dirt. In its heyday, El Mirador and all its surroundings may have embraced a population numbering some 80,000 souls.

Then suddenly, around AD 150, El Mirador fell into eclipse. Perhaps the crops failed; perhaps the ruling elite succumbed to conquest or rebellion. Whatever the reason, the site was abandoned, and the region's center of power shifted down to Tikal, some fifty miles to the south.

No Mayan site was more splendidly imposing than Tikal. Its soaring pyramids commanded the surrounding jungle. The carved monument stones of its central plaza would eventually describe six centuries of triumphant power. Like El Mirador, it served as a center of worship and administration for a surrounding community of peasant serfs. But with its resident hierarchies of priests, bureaucrats, scribes, artisans, and noblemen, the city's population may have reached 80,000 to 100,000.

Tikal's principal shrines also functioned as burial sites for its monarchs, who were laid out with great pomp and rich display in tombs cut into bedrock. Limestone temples marked the crypts. Some of the pyramids began as relatively small tombs. Then periodically, at times dictated by a succession to the throne or a congruence of planets, the city's architects erected larger stone buildings directly over the earlier ones, encasing them. The most prominent pyramids were designed from the beginning as very large tomb structures. These towers of dizzying steepness were richly carved with fantastic images of gods and humans, stuccoed over and painted in brilliant colors. The shrines at the peaks of the pyramids were roofed with corbel arches—false arches—in which each succeeding course of stones projected inward beyond the course below, until the arch culminated with the topmost stones from both sides abutting each other in the center. These simple structures were the only arches of any kind in the Americas. Tiara-like roof combs, elaborately carved and painted, crowned each shrine.

Tikal was only one of a dozen Mayan centers that, beginning around AD 200, arose in Mesoamerica. There was Lamanai in Belize, the site of huge pyramids; Copán in the hills of Honduras, with its handsome ball court and elegant stone statuary; Palenque and Bonampak in the Mexican jungles, their buildings ablaze with fine murals and carved glyphs; Dzibilchaltun on the Yucatán coast, a city of more than 100,000 that was a center of industry and crossroads of trade. Each was ruled by an independent royal dynasty that exercised power over surrounding territory. And each bore the characteristic stamp of Mayan artistic genius.

Mayan painters and sculptors depicted their subjects with a rigid system of symbolic representation, yet with flamboyant verve. Monarchs and gods, decked out in feathers and skins and festooned in ornaments of jade and shell, spilled out across the surfaces of stone and stucco as if no material limits could contain them. Flowers, birds, vines, animals, glyphs, and calendar notations swarmed in the background, merging and intertwining and spinning apart in frenzied mimicry of jungle life. Here, a warlord with a feathered cloak and an eagle headdress as big as himself strode the

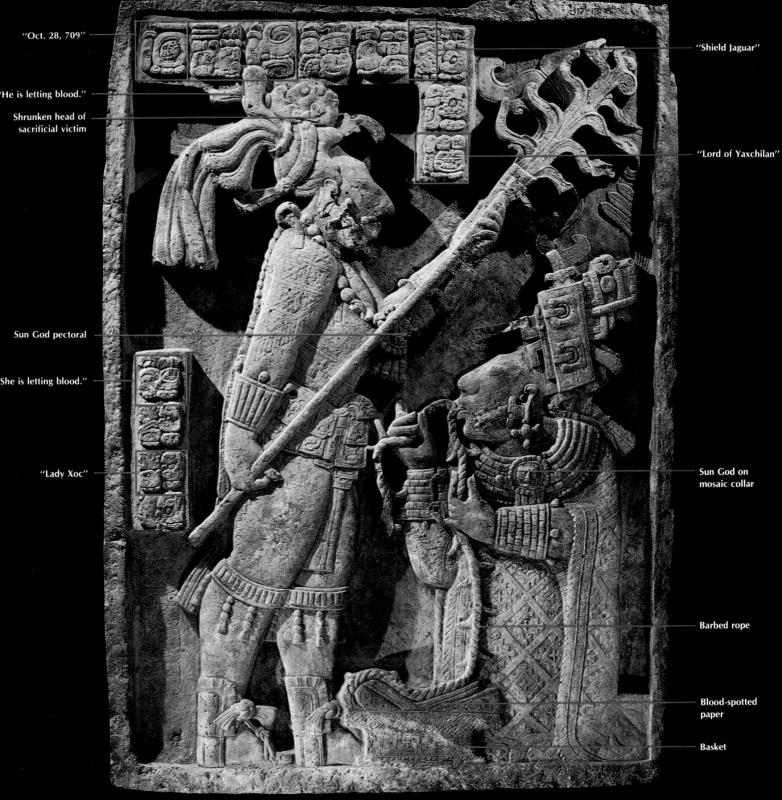

"Oct. 28, 709"

"He is letting blood."

Shrunken head of
sacrificial victim

Sun God pectoral

"She is letting blood."

"Lady Xoc"

"Shield Jaguar"

"Lord of Yaxchilan"

Sun God on
mosaic collar

Barbed rope

Blood-spotted
paper

Basket

backbone of the mythic plumed serpent. There, snails, turtles, and long-feathered tropical birds, magnificently drawn, participated in a cosmic dance. If the artists of Teotihuacán had a felicitous aptitude for geometric abstraction, the Maya were masters of baroque realism.

Accomplished farmers, inventive architects, impassioned embellishers, the Maya also had an unequaled flair for mathematics and astronomy. Their numerical system, expressed in dots and bars, was based on a count of twenty. When used in arithmetic calculations, it was far more supple and sophisticated than the Romans' awkward numbers. And, uniquely for that time, it included a zero, shown as a stylized shell.

The Maya used their numbers primarily to calculate and record dates. Their calendar incorporated several interlocking cycles of time. The most important were a solar year of 365 days and a ceremonial year that contained only 260 days; together these constituted what became known as "the Calendar Round." There were also the lunar cycle, the cycle of Venus, the Lords of the Night cycle, and the 819-day cycle. (The Maya left no clue as to the significance of the last two cycles.) The cycles ran concurrently, like meshed gears, and because the gears were of different sizes the alignment of the Calendar Round cycles would repeat only once every fifty-two years. For some other American cultures, a fifty-two-year calendar was sufficient—far longer, in fact, than most Stone Age lifetimes. But the Maya thought in spans of millennia, not years. They consequently developed what would be known as the Maya Long Count, which extended back to the day the earth was born—August 13, 3114 BC, by the modern Gregorian calendar—and looked ahead toward eternity. So distinctive were the numerical characteristics of each specific day that the same features could never recur; the calendar would go on endlessly with ever-longer cycles.

Mayan writing was no less elaborate. The script, the only complete writing system in America, combined pictograms with phonetic signs, much the way Chinese characters do. The image of a bat, for example, might indicate a real bat, pronounced *zotz* in the Mayan tongue. But it might also stand for the similar sound *tzi*—as in *tz'ib*, meaning "to write." This double service, applied to a language replete with synonyms and homonyms, allowed Mayan scribes to indulge a taste for fancy visual wordplay. In a stone inscription at Copán the name of a local lord, Smoke-Jaguar, is written in twenty different ways. Such scribal virtuosity was not unusual.

Insatiable record keepers, the Maya set down all events of dynastic or ceremonial importance. The accessions of kings, royal marriages, decisive military victories were all duly celebrated on monumental stone slabs in the city plazas. Administrative records and the astronomical tables that determined feast days and religious schedules were entered into fold-out, accordion-leaf books made of bark paper. (To make the paper, the Maya soaked pieces of a tree's inner bark to separate the fibers, and then pounded the fibers together into a smooth surface.) No works of classic Mayan literature would survive in their original form, but a compendium of myths, legends, history, religion, and astronomy known as the *Popol Vuh*, literally the "Book of the Community," was to be retranscribed by certain Mayan people not long after the Spanish conquest.

For all their intellectual sensitivity, the Maya could be savagely cruel and aggressive. Mayan men would march into battle with the passionate conviction of religious zealots—as indeed they were. Their primary purpose was not to conquer territory but to acquire captives for ritual sacrifice. And woe to the enemy who allowed himself to be taken. His death would be agonizingly slow, his bones pulled from their joints

In a relief from the Mayan palace complex at Yaxchilan, a kneeling woman, identified in the accompanying inscription as Lady Xoc, pulls a rope barbed with thorns through her tongue to draw blood; holding a flaring torch above the lady's head is her husband, a king called Shield-Jaguar, whose hair is adorned with the shrunken head of a sacrificial victim. Mayan kings and queens offered their blood to repay the gods for the divine sacrifices that nurtured the human race. The royal donors, weakened by the loss of blood, may have experienced visions that they interpreted as messages from the gods being honored.

and his body tormented with knives. In the end he would be decapitated, or his heart extracted with an obsidian knife.

If the sacrifice of an enemy was sweet to the Mayan gods, so also was the blood of Mayan rulers. Ritual bloodletting was a fundamental part of Mayan religion. Just as the gods poured out their life-giving sacred liquid, rain, to nourish the people, the Mayan rulers—who were believed to be descended from gods—gave their own vital sacred liquid, blood, to sustain the gods. (An analagous belief about the blood of a deity was central to the Christian ritual of the Eucharist, a religious practice that in this same time period was spreading in the Middle East and Europe.) To fulfill their bloodletting duties, Mayan kings and queens engaged in acts of self-mutilation, usually as part of important state events. One particularly painful method was to pull a length of thorn-studded twine through the tongue, catching the blood in a bowl. In another, a royal prince would spear his penis with the spine of a stingray.

A profound sense of the supernatural permeated every aspect of Mayan life. Each phenomenon of nature had its divine counterpart. The *Popol Vuh* told the story of two popular legendary figures known as the Hero Twins, Hunahpú and Xbalanqué, who excelled as blowgun marksmen and as ball players. In one ball game, they faced off

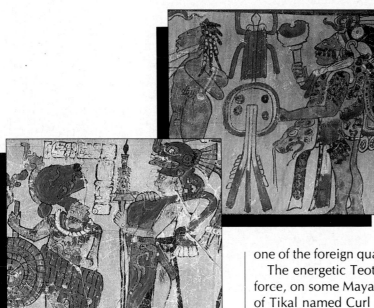

against the Lords of the Underworld, grim opponents who each bore the name of a fatal disease. By trickery, the Hero Twins triumphed and rose up to heaven to become the sun and the moon. Several deities were apparently borrowed from Central Mexico: the Plumed Serpent, which the Maya called Kukulcán, and the goggle-eyed Tlaloc, known in the Yucatán as Chaac, and here associated with blood sacrifices as well as rain.

During the fifth and sixth centuries, when the cultures of the Maya and of the Teotihuacanos both were at their peaks, strong reciprocal currents flowed between the Mayan communities and the great imperial city in the north. The exchange was both spiritual and commercial. Obsidian tools, ceramic tripod vases, and the ubiquitous thin orange pottery of the Cholula area all found their way into the Mayan jungles along with the Teotihuacano gods. And one of the foreign quarters in the Mexican capital was given over to Mayan residents.

The energetic Teotihuacanos may have exerted political influence, perhaps even force, on some Mayan centers in the interest of trade. In the fifth century, a monarch of Tikal named Curl Nose was depicted on a monument stone in the central plaza wearing Teotihuacano costume. But by the year 600 the influence of Teotihuacán began to fade. In Tikal and its neighboring centers, not a single monument stone had been erected in half a century. This lapse of endeavor may have coincided with the gradual withdrawal of the Teotihuacanos. A political vacuum would have resulted, causing the disruption of the customary rites and ceremonies at Tikal. In other regions as well, the might of the Mexican Valley was in slow decline.

Several factors might have contributed to the weakening of Teotihuacán: a population grown too large for its agricultural base, an episode of political instability, a change in climate bringing drought and crop failure. Vast quantities of firewood were necessary to burn the lime used for coating Teotihuacán's pyramids and apartment buildings, and the overcutting of trees could have denuded the valley's natural

At top, a Mayan warrior wearing a pelt and carrying a mace and a staff ushers a captive off to his fate. Above, another prisoner—this one a defeated lord with a headdress, a broken staff, and a rope around his neck—kneels before his counterpart. The capture of even low-ranking men was a point of pride among the Maya, since the prisoner's lifeblood could be offered to the gods. But taking a dignitary was of greater consequence: Captive kings might be kept alive for repeated bloodlettings.

As suggested by their trappings, Mayan warriors considered battle more as a ceremony than as a means of resolving disputes. The shells covering the breast of the clay figure at right, from the Gulf coast island of Jaina, would have offered the warrior little protection in a fight; but like his facial markings and deer headdress, they formed part of the proud costume of an actor in a ritualized drama. Similarly, the plumage and staff ornaments of the warrior below served little practical purpose other than to mark him as a participant in a solemn pageant, enacted to satisfy the gods.

watersheds and eroded the surrounding hillsides. For whatever reason, the empire became increasingly vulnerable.

The end came around 750, in a fiery cataclysm worthy of the city's mythical origins. The sanctuaries and palaces along the Avenue of the Dead were put to the torch. The destroyers, whoever they were, hacked away the grand staircase of the Pyramid of the Moon. They threw down the ceremonial platforms and uprooted the sculpted columns of the nearby Palace of the Quetzal Butterfly, burying the rubble in a large pit. When they finally ceased their devastating work, the ceremonial and administrative heart of the city lay in ruin. In the resulting chaos, the inhabitants—the ones who survived—abandoned Teotihuacán for hardscrabble settlements in the countryside.

Eventually, the great Mayan centers would also collapse, although that fall would be almost two centuries in coming. Meanwhile, the cities in the Petén jungle enjoyed a resurgence of energy and development. The builders at Tikal resumed their work; new sets of monument stones inscribed tales of victories and accessions, and the city's pyramids rose to even greater heights above the forest. The sculptors at Palenque and the mural painters at Bonampak strove for and achieved new splendors of imagery and skill. Mayan cultural influence, perhaps carried by traders, spread northward into the territory that once had been dominated by Teotihuacán. Cosmopolitan centers bearing the unmistakable hallmarks of Mayan artistic inspiration took shape at Cacaxtla northeast of Cholula and on the terraced hilltop of Xochicalco just below the southern perimeter of the Valley of Mexico.

But during the ninth century the Mayan world declined precipitously, perhaps as a result of the same kind of political and environmental decay that seem to have weakened Teotihuacán. The intensive farming in the Petén may have impoverished the soil and rendered it infertile. Diseases of malnutrition, such as rickets, beset the common people, although the city elite went on eating well enough. Tension between a starving peasantry and a callous aristocracy may have sparked discontent and ignited rebellion. Inexorably, the jungle cities began to lose their magic. The cult ceremonies ended as the rulers and priests moved elsewhere. And by AD 900, the forest would begin relentlessly creeping in, shrouding the shrines and monuments in a dense green tangle.

On first inspection, western Peru would have seemed an unlikely place for civilization to take hold and thrive. The apparent barriers to progress there could hardly have been more intimidating. A strip of desert along the Pacific coast, where rain might not fall for a century or more, rose to barren hillsides cut by steep river valleys. Above these loomed the Andes Mountains, a cool realm of tablelands, rocky terrain, and some fertile valleys surrounded by glacial ice and peaks soaring up to 22,000 feet above sea level.

Yet civilization had long existed throughout this unpromising region. The coastal deserts bordered one of the world's richest fishing grounds, and the chill Pacific waters provided a bountiful harvest for scores of local villages. They hauled in anchovies by the ton to be dried and ground into protein-rich meal, nourishing as a key food and easy to preserve and transport as a staple of trade. Advances in irrigation techniques had fostered the spread of farming communities along the river valleys, turning them into green ribbons of fertility wending across the desert. Higher up, the sparse tableland grasses offered adequate grazing for alpacas and vicuñas, raised

The surefooted llama—portrayed here balancing a ceramic vessel—was vital to trade along the rugged trails that led from the coast of present-day Peru up through the high passes of the Andes to the dense jungle beyond. Too slight to be ridden, the animal was saddled with light loads and led in trains by merchants traveling from village to village. In addition, the llama yielded a coarse wool and could be slaughtered for leather or meat—serving the people of the region so well that some of them worshiped its image.

mainly for their wool, and llamas, used as pack animals and as a source of meat. From the mountains came metals—gold, silver, and copper, which a number of peoples in the region learned to work into ornaments and tools.

The most pervasive culture here prior to this period had been that of the Chavín. In a narrow valley 10,200 feet above sea level in central Peru stood the monumental stone sanctuary of the Chavín jaguar god, casting the spell of its stern cult from the mountains to the coast. Like their distant contemporaries, Mesoamerica's Olmecs, the people of the Chavín culture had helped to set the course for their successors. A number of Peruvian groups took inspiration from the Chavín example. Images of the snarling jaguar deity, with clenched teeth and overlapping fangs, continued to appear on pottery and textiles for centuries after the original cult had faded. At different times, the artisans at Huari in the mountains, at Lima and Paracas on the coast, and as far south as Lake Titicaca in the upper reaches of the Andes Massif, all worked with Chavín motifs. But nowhere was the influence more striking than among the people who dwelt in the Moche River valley of northern Peru.

At first there was little to distinguish the Moche from the peoples of neighboring valleys. Moche fishermen braved the ocean currents in canoelike rafts made from bundles of reeds lashed together, hauling in catches of anchovy, crab, and shrimp. Moche farmers grew a wide assortment of South American staples in irrigated fields along the river. Corn was the major crop, as in other communities, and it had a multitude of uses. The Moche ate it on the cob, either roasted or steamed. They pressed oil from the kernels or fermented them into beer. From the stalks they extracted a sweet juice for drinking. They also cultivated and ate green beans and lima beans, white potatoes and sweet potatoes, peppers, peanuts, manioc, numerous squashes and gourds, and such fruits as guava, avocado, papaya, and pineapple. And they raised a great deal of cotton, much of it for trade. Natural stands of giant reeds, cana brava, provided construction material and fiber for baskets.

All this was achieved with considerable effort. The Moche worked long and hard to maintain their irrigation canals; the March rainy season and thaw in the uplands could bring floods and mud slides downstream, while in October the river might dry up and disappear entirely. On the other hand, the region was blessed with a virtually inexhaustible supply of fertilizer. Just off the coast was a string of islands smothered in guano dropped by seabirds; Moche farmers plastered it on their fields, making the soil wonderfully rich.

Although fish were plentiful, meat tended to be scarce. Farmers in the valley raised ducks and guinea pigs for the dinner pot; highland families could butcher a llama if they did not need it for a pack animal. Wild game was at a premium. A hungry villager might bring down a bird or two with a blowgun, but the deer that roamed the upland plateaus were reserved for the tribal aristocracy. Hunting them was a

Amazon River

Moche

A N D E S

PERU

Lima

Huari

Paracas

Nazca

Lake Titicaca

PACIFIC OCEAN

matter of much ceremony and organization, with teams of dogs and beaters driving the quarry into nets, there to be speared by richly clad noblemen.

Life in an early Moche community was normally a simple affair, however. Most villagers lived in one-room houses of mud-daubed reeds supported by wooden corner posts—although wealthier people might build homes of adobe brick. A cluster of adobe mounds around a central plaza marked a ceremonial precinct that was occupied by only a few priests, except on ritual occasions, when the villagers gathered there. Like all Peruvians, the Moche loved music and dancing, and they exuberantly filled the mountain air with the pipings of bone flutes and pottery whistles, the boom of conch shells and ceramic trumpets, and the percussive rhythms of drums, rattles, and tambourines.

Industrious traders, villagers on the coast shipped guano to the farmers up river. In return they received produce and metal tools. Another commodity imported from the mountains was coca, whose narcotic leaf was chewed with lime to counteract feelings of fatigue.

Early in the second century AD, the Moche seem to have experienced a sudden surge in cultural progress. They expanded their irrigation system to bring more land under cultivation and proved themselves to be master hydrologists. Led on by increasingly powerful rulers, they constructed a network of aqueducts, reservoirs, and channels that would remain in use long after the last member of Moche society had faded into obscurity. One mile-long ditch ran along the crest of a huge earthen embankment fifty feet above the valley floor. Another canal stretched a full seventy-five miles from the water source to the farthest fields. Such control over water led to increasingly bountiful harvests and a consequent rising population. More people meant more mouths to feed—and a craving for still more land.

And so the Moche began to push their way into adjacent valleys. They absorbed the neighboring Gallinazo culture, which had preceded their own rise to prominence, and then edged out along the coast in both directions. Eventually they controlled a territory covering some 500 miles of Peru's northern coast and extending inland to the Andes.

While the urge to expand was partly economic, another impetus was religion. An important Moche deity, perhaps their supreme god, was the Chavín jaguar god reincarnated: Fierce and imperious, he sat enthroned in the mountains, ruling the sky and all creation. But he sent his look-alike deputy, the sun, to subdue the lowlands. The deputy hunted for deer, caught fish and seabirds, and embarked on a reed raft to battle the crab monster who lived in the ocean depths. Invariably, the sun won, for he was a brave and powerful god. And like other American deities, he seems to have enjoyed the sacrificial offering of human life.

The Moche obliged him. When they went to war, armed with stout maces and copper-headed axes and clad in brightly colored helmets and cotton tunics, they made certain to bring back captives for sacrificial victims. Some captives were hurled over precipices—offerings for the senior sky deity. But most were stripped naked, roped together, and led to the great plaza at Moche, the Moche's principal ceremonial site. Then their captors would slit their throats or lop off their heads. Captured noblemen were given special treatment, for the Moche maintained a fine sense of class distinction. While common soldiers walked to the executioner's block, their superiors were carried there in litters.

The Moche ceremonial site was one of the grandest of its era and an imposing testament to its builders' growing power. One Moche pyramid—much later dubbed the Pyramid of the Sun by the Spanish—was a gigantic structure built of some 50 million sun-baked adobe bricks that rose in tiers to a height of perhaps 150 feet. It looked out across an open expanse to a large natural hill, below which stood a somewhat more modest pyramid the Spanish were to call the Pyramid of the Moon. Both structures contained large rooms with colorfully frescoed walls. On one wall of the Pyramid of the Moon, artists painted an astonishing army of animated clay pots and utensils that were marching about brandishing weapons, as if in revolt against their workaday status.

For all their combative disposition, the Moche were remarkably sensitive practitioners of the arts. Chavín metalsmiths had worked for many centuries in the Andes, pioneering techniques for hammering ornaments from gold and silver. Copper had also seen long use, for ornaments as well as mace heads and lance points and the points of digging sticks. But the Moche surpassed all their Peruvian metalworking predecessors in both skill and imagination. Smelting ores in clay ovens, probably with some kind of forced draft arrangement to make the charcoal fires burn hot, they fashioned copper masks and gold earspools inlaid with shell and turquoise, helmets

Carved on the sun-burnished surface of the desert plateau above the Nazca Valley, this stylized hummingbird—whose beak alone extends for 120 feet—stands as a tribute to the precision of the engineers who plotted the design and the perseverance of the laborers who executed it. Associated with the dazzling power of the sun, hummingbirds were often portrayed on Nazca pots as well. This monumental ground drawing was one of scores of such designs—including eighteen bird figures—fashioned on the plateau so that they could be seen in full only from aloft; they may have been intended for the enjoyment of the gods, who, like the birds themselves or the circling stars, were free of the earth and could perceive things hidden to humans.

and headdresses of beaten gold, gold bracelets and nose rings, and diminutive, hammered-gold statues.

They devised for themselves a lost-wax method of casting hollow metal figures, similar to the technique that had been used on the other side of the world since the third millennium BC. They began by creating a heat-resistant model of clay mixed with carbon, then coated it with a thin layer of wax, sculpting details into the wax layer's surface. Next they applied a layer of heat-proof clay over the wax, making two carefully positioned holes through the clay before it hardened. When molten metal was poured into one of the holes in this outer mold, it melted the wax and pushed it out the other hole. After the metal hardened, the clay molds were broken to remove the newly cast figure.

The supreme achievement of Moche artisans, however, was their pottery. They made flasks with ingenious stirrup-shaped handles that also served as spouts, pitchers that whistled (because air was sucked in through tiny vents as the liquid was poured out), beakers in the shape of animals and gods, beakers that looked like bunches of corn or mounds of potatoes, ceramic portraits of handsome nobles with tattooed faces. They painted most of the vessels, coloring some to enhance sculptural effects, depicting scenes from tribal life on others. Warriors battled across the ceramic surfaces, revelers danced, hunters stalked deer, and tribal lords chewed coca under a starry sky. They traded their pottery widely, shipping it all along the coast and to tribes in the Andes highlands.

These were no ordinary pots; some of them would survive for millennia, undimmed as resplendent masterpieces of ceramic art. The potters seemed to instill every nuance of experience and desire into their work. They could be witty or serene, majestic or crude, homey or imperial as occasion demanded. They clearly intended some items to inspire religious awe: grimacing portraits of a god with heavy-lidded eyes, for instance, snakes darting from ears and hair. Others depicted sexual scenes—some tenderly romantic, some overtly bawdy.

Enterprising though they were, the Moche never expanded much beyond the northern sector of Peru's coastline. Meanwhile, along the ocean some 600 miles to the south, another people were building themselves a civilization. These were the Nazca. They lived in adjoining river valleys where desert met sea, in grass-thatch villages clustered around adobe pyramids of relatively modest size. They fished, hunted, and tended the usual crops on irrigated desert soil. When they went to war, the Nazca took heads as battle trophies. Headhunting was an ancient preoccupation of the Andean region. Its early practitioners had included a tribe of fishermen—direct cultural ancestors of the Nazca—who dwelt on the Paracas Peninsula, a barren and windswept spit of sand jutting out into the Pacific.

The Paracas people had devoted much energy to matters of death and the afterlife, and they wove extravagant burial shrouds. Theirs were among the finest textiles produced anywhere in the world. Embroidered in cotton and wool of rainbow hues, the fabric showed as its most striking motif a bizarre deity who had dangling limbs and was festooned with trophy heads. He was portrayed with great, staring eyes, which would inspire archaeologists much later to dub him the Oculate Being.

The Nazca inherited the Oculate Being from the Paracas culture. Like the Paracas people, they paid homage to that deity, wove beautiful fabric for shrouds, and buried their dead in a distinctive manner. They placed the body in a squatting position, knees against chest, and bound it in many yards of cloth, sometimes wrapping clothing, gold ornaments, feather fans, and food offerings into the bundle with the deceased. The Nazca then buried the body in a circular pit; the Paracas people put the wrapped corpse in a basket and interred it in an underground tomb constructed of adobe bricks.

Another unusual practice the Nazca inherited was trepanning—the cutting open of a living person's skull. A priest or medicine man would remove a piece of the subject's cranium, by drilling a hole or cutting out a rectangle or simply scraping away at the bared bone after removing part of the skin. In many cases, the operation apparently had no lasting ill effects. The bone simply grew back, and a number of subjects were trepanned several times. The Nazca left no explanation as to why they practiced trepanning. In a culture that battled with war clubs, bashed skulls must have been an all-too-frequent occurrence; the operation may have been an attempt to repair some of the damage.

The Nazca probably equalled their Paracas forebears in textile making. (They wove designs into their fabrics, instead of embroidering them as the Paracas people did.) And they outshone the earlier culture in the art of ceramics. Nazca potters shared a number of traits with the Moche masters—sculpting images of people and beasts and employing brightly painted decorations. But the Nazca tended to create simpler shapes. They painted their pottery with a bolder hand more inclined to geometric designs, and their subjects were largely symbolic.

The crowning achievement of Nazca creativity, however, was on a far larger, almost superhuman, scale. They were artists in gravel and sand, and their canvas was the mighty sweep of the desert itself, a stretch of flat, barren plain between the Nazca and Ingenio river valleys. There, successive generations traced out a series of enormous figures, removing the dark, weathered surface gravel to reveal the lighter, contrasting gravel beneath and delineating the edges of the patterns with piled rocks and gravel. They took some of their early designs from nature, including dolphins, a giant bird, and a monkey with a great swirling tail. About three dozen of the pictures were of this type. But a later generation of Nazca artists were pure abstractionists, creating only spirals and zigzags, trapezoids and triangles, and webs of arrow-straight lines that often radiated from sand hummocks and extended for up to eight miles. The artists created some 300 geometrical figures, spread out across 4.3 million square yards of desert.

Most of the drawings were too large to be seen whole from ground level, and the nearest hills would have provided only an unsatisfactory distant view. The pictures may have had astronomical significance. Some of the lines were aligned with key celestial references, and the depicted animals played roles in Nazca myths about heavenly bodies. Perhaps the figures formed a great terrestial zodiac, by which the Nazca determined the times to plant their seeds and open the floodgates of their irrigation ditches. Or maybe the artists intended some other purpose for the lines— to serve as processional avenues to desert shrines or simply as intricately patterned pathways that, when walked, would amuse the person using them or invite some other mood or insight.

Like the enigma of trepanning, the Nazca lines would provoke much speculation by future scholars—and not only scholars, but peoples of other cultures who later would occupy the land. The time would soon come when the Moche and Nazca, for all their brilliance and battlefield valor, would yield hegemony over the region to other nations who would rise to power in the second half of the first millennium.

600 BC — AD 199	AD 200	AD 250	AD 300	AD 350

ROMAN EMPIRE

| | | Emperor Diocletian takes control of the Roman Empire. | Constantine I calls the first Ecumenical Council at Nicaea in Asia Minor.

Under Constantine I, Constantinople becomes the "new Rome," the eastern capital of the Roman Empire. | Visigoths appeal to the Romans for refuge from the Huns.

Christianity becomes the state religion under Theodosius I. |

INDIA AND PERSIA

| 78-101 Kanishka is ruler of the Kushan empire in India. | The Persian Ardashir defeats the last Parthian king and establishes the Sassanian empire in Persia. | Shapur I of Persia captures the Roman emperor Valerian. | Under Shapur II, Persia captures parts of the Roman Empire but loses Armenia to the White Huns.

Chandra Gupta I starts northern India's Gupta era. | Chandra Gupta II reigns in India.

India's two greatest epic poems, *Ramayana* and *Mahabharata*, appear in final Sanskrit form. |

CHINA AND SOUTHEAST ASIA

| AD 100 Funan becomes a kingdom in the Mekong Delta. | China has civil war period with three empires in control: the Wei kingdom in the north, the Shu in the west, and the Wu in the south.

China sends an emissary to Funan and trades with the city of Oc Eo. | The Jin dynasty succeeds the Wei and absorbs the Wu. | Turkish and Mongol barbarians invade China and create sixteen kingdoms in the north. South China remains apart with its own dynasties. | The Wei dynasty in the north unifies North China in 439 and establishes the capital at Luoyang in 494. |

AMERICAS

| 600-400 BC The Paracas culture produces embroidered textiles and buries its dead in baskets.

400 BC-AD 540 Nazca people make multicolored pottery and crisscross the desert with huge animal designs.

400 BC Monte Albán becomes the political capital and ceremonial center of the Zapotec nation and remains so until about AD 800. | | | 300-600 Heyday of the Moche people in northern Peru. | |

TimeFrame: AD 200-600

AD 400	AD 450	AD 500	AD 550	AD 600
Vandals attack across the Rhine into Roman Gaul and move into Spain by 409.	Roman troops, with Visigothic and other allies, defeat Attila at the Battle of Catalaunian Fields. Attila retreats, then invades northern Italy.	Clovis defeats the Visigoths and drives them toward Spain.		
Alaric the Visigoth captures Rome.		The Frankish kingdom is divided among Clovis's four sons.		
The Romans grant the Visigoths a settlement in southern Gaul.	Vandals raid and plunder Rome.	Justin I becomes the Byzantine emperor.		
The Vandals move from Spain into northern Africa.	Theodoric becomes king of the Ostrogoths. He invades Italy in 489.	Justinian rules over the Eastern Roman Empire.		
St. Patrick begins mission in Ireland to spread Christianity.	Clovis, king of the Franks, defeats the Roman general of northern Gaul and takes his place.	Construction begins on the basilica of St. Sophia in Constantinople.	Lombards invade northern Italy.	
Attila rules as king of the Huns.		Justinian's army conquers the Vandal kingdom in North Africa and gradually crushes Ostrogoth resistance in Italy.	Gregory the Great is elected pope. In 597 he sends missionaries to England to convert the Anglo-Saxons.	
Angles, Saxons, and Jutes colonize Britain.				

Chinese Buddhist Faxian makes a pilgrimage to India and writes an account of his travels.				
The Indian poet Kalidasa writes the play *Shakuntala* and other Sanskrit works.				
Kumara Gupta takes over the Indian throne.	Skanda Gupta, last of the important Gupta kings, defeats the White Huns.	Chosroes I reunites Persia.		

	King Jayavarman of Funan asks China's help in conquering the neighboring kingdom of Linyi.			
	Buddhism grows in China with the building of cave temples at Yungang and Longmen.			

		The Teotihuacán civilization peaks in the Valley of Mexico.		
		500-900 The city of El Tajín in Veracruz builds many courts for ball games.		600-800 Temple pyramids are built by Mayas at the cities of Tikal, Palenque, and Copán.

INDEX

ACKNOWLEDGMENTS

The editors wish to thank the following individuals and institutions for their valuable assistance in the preparation of this volume:
ENGLAND: London—Department of Oriental Antiquities, British Museum; T. C. Mitchell, Keeper of Western Asiatic Antiquities, British Museum; T. W. Potter, Department of Prehistoric and Romano-British Antiquities, British Museum; Anthony Shelton, Department of Ethnography, British Museum; Brian A. Tremain, Photographic Service, British Museum; Susan M. Youngs, Department of Medieval and Later Antiquities, British Museum.
FEDERAL REPUBLIC OF GERMANY: Berlin—Edmund Buchner, President, Deutsches Archaeologisches Institut; Dieter Eisleb, Direktor, Museum für Völkerkunde, Staatliche Museen Preussischer Kulturbesitz; Heidi Klein, Bildarchiv Preussischer Kulturbesitz; Karl Heinz Pütz, Direktor, Bildarchiv Preussischer Kulturbesitz; Lore Sander, Museum für Indische Kunst, Staatliche Museen Preussischer Kulturbesitz; Hans-Georg Severin, Direktor, Frühchristlich-Byzantinische Abteilung, Staatliche Museen Preussischer Kulturbesitz; Marianne Yaldiz, Direktor, Museum für Indische Kunst, Staatliche Museen Preussischer Kulturbesitz. Cologne—Gisela Völger, Direktor, Rautenstrauch-Joest Museum für Völkerkunde. Munich—Ferdinand Anton; Irmgard Ernstmeier, Hirmer Verlag; Hans Peter Hilger, Bayerisches Nationalmuseum; Helmut Schindler, Museum für Völkerkunde; Dietrich Wildung, Direktor, Staatliche Sammlung Ägyptischer Kunst. Passau—Helmut Bender, Universität Passau, Institut für Provincial-Römische Archaeologie. Stockdorf—Claus Hansmann, Kulturgeschichtliches Bildarchiv. Stuttgart—Klaus-J. Brandt, Linden Museum; Hilmar Schickler, Württembergisches Landesmuseum; Axel Schulze-Thulin, Linden Museum. Trier—Hartwig Löhr, Rheinisches Landesmuseum; Hans Nortmann, Rheinisches Landesmuseum.
FRANCE: Paris—François Avril, Curateur, Département des Manuscripts, Bibliothèque Nationale; Christophe Barbotin, Conservateur du Département des Antiquités Egyptiennes, Musée du Louvre; Laure Beaumont-Maillet, Conservateur en Chef du Cabinet des Estampes, Bibliothèque Nationale; Catherine Bélanger, Chargée des Relations Extérieures du Musée du Louvre; Jeannette Chalufour, Archives Tallandier; Béatrice Coti, Directrice du Service Iconographique, Editions Mazenod; Antoinette Decaudin, Documentaliste, Département des Antiquités Orientales, Musée du Louvre; Michel Fleury, Président de la IV Section de l'École Pratique des Hautes Études; Marie-Françoise Huygues des Étages, Conservateur, Musée de la Marine; Françoise Jestaz, Conservateur, Cabinet des Estampes, Bibliothéque Nationale; Marie Montembault, Documentaliste, Département des Antiquités Grecques et Romaines, Musée du Louvre; Marie-Odile Roy, Service Photographique, Bibliothèque Nationale; Jacqueline Sanson, Conservateur, Directeur du Service Photographique, Bibliothèque Nationale; Madanjeet Singh, Art Historian.
GERMAN DEMOCRATIC REPUBLIC: Berlin—Arne Effenberger, Direktor, Frühchristlich-Byzantinische Sammlung, Staatliche Museen zu Berlin.

IRELAND: Dublin—Michael Herity, Department of Archaeology, University College.
ITALY: Florence—Brigitte Baumbusch, Scala. Milan—Frederico Borromeo; Luisa Ricciarini. Rome—Suora Maria Francesca Antongiovanni, Catacombe di Priscilla; Principe Alessandro Torlonia, Amministrazione Torlonia.
SWEDEN: Gothenburg—Gunilla Amnehall, Conservator of Textiles, Göteborg Etnografiska Museum.
TURKEY: Istanbul—Emin Baranbilek, Assistant Director of the Archeological Museum; Sirasi Basegmez, Hagia Sophia Museum; Alpaslan Koyunlu, Restoration Director, Hagia Sophia Museum; Wolfgang Muller-Weiner, German Archeology Institute; Alpay Pasinli, Director, Archeological Museum; Erdem Yucel, Director, Hagia Sophia Museum.
U.S.A.: New Hampshire: Lyme—Wango Weng. New York: New York City—Marilyn Wong-Glysteen, Assistant Professor, Chinese Art, Columbia University. Washington, D.C.: William Loerke, Professor of Byzantine Art, Dumbarton Oaks and Visiting Professor, History of Architecture, Catholic University of America.

The index for this volume was prepared by Roy Nanovic.

BIBLIOGRAPHY

BOOKS

Alkazi, Roshen, *Ancient Indian Costume.* New Delhi: E. Alkazi for Art Heritage, 1983.

Anton, Ferdinand, *The Art of Ancient Peru.* New York: G. P. Putnam's Sons, 1972.

Asimov, Isaac, *Constantinople: The Forgotten Empire.* Boston: Houghton Mifflin, 1970.

Bankes, George, *Moche Pottery from Peru.* London: British Museum Publications Ltd., 1980.

Barnes, Timothy D., *Constantine and Eusebius.* Cambridge, Mass.: Harvard University Press, 1981.

Barraclough, Geoffrey, ed., *The Times Atlas of World History.* Maplewood, N.J.: Hammond Inc., 1979.

Bary, William Theodore de, ed., *Sources of Chinese Tradition.* New York: Columbia University Press, 1960.

Basham, A. L., *The Wonder That Was India.* New York: Hawthorn Books, 1963.

Beckwith, John, *Early Christian and Byzantine Art.* Harmondsworth, Middlesex, England: Penguin Books, 1986.

Benson, Elizabeth P., *The Mochica.* New York: Praeger, 1972.

Berlo, Janet Catherine, *Teotihuacan Art Abroad* (BAR International Series 199 (i)). Oxford: B.A.R., 1984.

Biswas, Atreyi, *The Political History of the Hūnas in India.* New Delhi: Munshiram Manoharlal Publishers Pvt. Ltd., 1973.

Brauer, George C., Jr., *The Age of the Soldier Emperors.* Park Ridge, N.J.: Noyes Press, 1975.

Breasted, James Henry, *Oriental Forerunners of Byzantine Painting.* Vol. 1. Chicago: The University of Chicago Press, 1924.

Brown, Peter:
Augustine of Hippo. Berkeley, Calif.: University of California Press, 1975.
The World of Late Antiquity. New York: Harcourt Brace Jovanovich, 1971.

Buchanan, Keith, Charles P. FitzGerald, and Colin A. Ronan, *China.* New York: Crown Publishers, 1981.

Burns, Thomas S., *A History of the Ostrogoths.* Bloomington, Ind.: Indiana University Press, 1984.

Bushnell, G. H. S., *Peru* (Ancient Peoples and Places series). New York: Frederick A. Praeger, 1963.

Byvanck, A. W., *L'Art de Constantinople.* Leiden, Holland: L. Byvanck-Quarles van Ufford, 1977.

The Cambridge Ancient History. Vol. 12, *The Imperial Crisis and Recovery: A.D. 193-324.* Ed. by S. A. Cook, et al. Cambridge: Cambridge University Press, 1939.

The Cambridge Medieval History. Vol. 1, *The Christian Roman Empire and the Foundation of the Teutonic Kingdoms.* Ed. by J. B. Bury, H. M. Gwatkin, and J. P. Whitney. London: Cambridge University Press, 1975.

Campbell, James, Eric John, and Patrick Wormald, *The Anglo-Saxons.* Ithaca, N.Y.: Cornell University Press / Phaidon Books, 1982.

Campbell, Leroy A., *Mithraic Iconography and Ideology.* Leiden, Holland: E. J. Brill, 1968.

Capon, Edmond, *Art & Archaeology in China.* South Melbourne, Australia: The Macmillan Co. of Australia Pty. Ltd., 1977.

Cary, M., and H. H. Scullard, *A History of Rome.* New York: St. Martin's Press, 1975.

Chadwick, Henry, *The Early Church.* Harmondsworth, Middlesex, England: Penguin Books, 1971.

Ch'en, Kenneth K. S., *Buddhism in China: A Historical Survey.* Princeton, N.J.: Princeton University Press, 1964.

Coe, Michael D.:
The Maya (Ancient Peoples and Places series). London: Thames and Hudson, 1987.
Mexico (Ancient Peoples and Places series). London: Thames and Hudson, 1984.

Coe, Michael D., Dean Snow, and Elizabeth Benson, *Atlas of Ancient America.* New York: Facts on File Publications, 1986.

Coedès, G., *The Indianized States of Southeast Asia.* Transl. by Susan Brown Cowing. Honolulu: East-West Center Press, 1968.

Cordy-Collins, Alana, and Jean Stern, *Pre-Columbian Art History.* Palo Alto, Calif.: Peek Publications, 1977.

Cornell, Tim, and John Matthews, *Atlas of the Roman World.* New York: Facts on File, Inc., 1983.

Davies, Nigel, *The Ancient Kingdoms of Mexico.* Harmondsworth, Middlesex, England: Penguin Books, 1985.

Dickey, Thomas, Vance Muse, and Henry Wiencek, *The God-Kings of Mexico* (Treasures of the World series). Chicago: Stonehenge Press Inc., 1982.

Didron, Adolphe Napolèon, *Christian Iconography: The History of Christian Art in the Middle Ages.* Vols. 1 and 2. Transl. by E. J. Millington. New York: Frederick Ungar, 1965.

Diehl, Charles, *Justinien et la Civilisation Byzantine au VIe Siècle.* Vols. 1 and 2. New York: Burt Franklin, 1969.

Diesner, Hans-Joachim, *The Great Migration.* New York: Hippocrene Books, 1982.

Donnan, Christopher B., *Moche Art of Peru: Pre-Columbian Symbolic Communication.* Los Angeles: Museum of Cultural History, University of California, 1978.

Downey, Glanville, *Constantinople in the Age of Justinian.* Norman, Okla.: University of Oklahoma Press, 1960.

Dumbarton Oaks Papers. Nos. 18 and 23. Washington, D.C.: The Dumbarton Oaks Center for Byzantine Studies / Trustees for Harvard University, 1964.

Eberhard, Wolfram, *A History of China.* Berkeley, Calif.: University of California Press, 1969.

Ebrey, Patricia Buckley, *The Aristocratic Families of Early Imperial China.* Cambridge: Cambridge University Press, 1978.

Ebrey, Patricia Buckley, ed., *Chinese Civilization and Society.* New York: The Free Press, 1981.

Effenberger, Arne, *Koptische Kunst.* Leipzig, East Germany: Koehler & Amelang, 1975.

Fairbank, John K., Edwin O. Reischauer, and Albert M. Craig, *East Asia Tradition and Transformation.* Boston: Houghton Mifflin, 1973.

Ferrill, Arther, *The Fall of the Roman Empire: The Military Explanation.* London: Thames and Hudson, 1986.

Forsyth, George H., and Kurt Weitzmann, *The Monastery of Saint Catherine at Mount Sinai: The Church and Fortress of Justinian.* Ann Arbor, Mich.: The University of Michigan Press, 1973.

Fossati, Gildo, *China* (The Monuments of Civilization series). Transl. by Bruce Penman. Kent, England: New English Library, 1983.

Frye, Richard N., *The Heritage of Persia.* London: Readers Union / Weidenfeld and Nicolson, 1964.

Gernet, Jacques, *A History of Chinese Civilization.* Transl. by J. R. Foster. Cambridge: Cambridge University Press, 1985.

Ghirshman, Roman:
Iran: From the Earliest Times to the Islamic Conquest. Harmondsworth, Middlesex, England: Penguin Books, 1961.
Persian Art: The Parthian and Sassanian Dynasties: 249 B.C.–A.D. 65. Transl. by Stuart Gilbert and James Emmons. New York: Golden Press, 1962.

Giles, H. A., transl., *The Travels of Fah-sien (399-414 A.D.), or Record of Buddhistic Kingdoms.* Cambridge: Cambridge University Press, 1923.

Goffart, Walter, *Barbarians and Romans.* Princeton, N.J.: Princeton University Press, 1980.

Goodenough, Erwin R., *Symbolism in the Dura Synagogue.* Vols. 9, 10, and 11 of *Jewish Symbols in the Greco-Roman Period.* New York: Bollingen Foundation, 1964.

Goodrich, L. Carrington, *A Short History of the Chinese People.* New York: Harper & Brothers Publishers, 1959.

Gough, Michael, *The Origins of Christian Art.* New York: Praeger, 1974.

Grabar, André, *The Golden Age of Justinian.* Transl. by Stuart Gilbert and James Emmons. New York: Odyssey Press, 1967.

Griffin, John, *The Paintings in the Buddhist Cave-Temples of Ajanta.* Vol. 1. Delhi: Caxton Publications, 1983.

Gutmann, Joseph, ed., *The Dura-Europos Synagogue: A Re-evaluation (1932-1972).* Missoula, Montana: American Academy of Religion / Society of Biblical Literature, 1973.

Hall, D. G. E., *A History of South-East Asia.* New York: St. Martin's Press, 1981.

Hammond, Norman, *Ancient Maya Civilization.* New Brunswick, N.J.: Rutgers University Press, 1982.

Hopkins, Clark, *The Discovery of Dura-Europos.* New Haven, Conn.: Yale University Press, 1979.

Hotz, Walter, *Byzanz, Konstantinopel, Istanbul.* Munich, West Germany: Deutscher Kunstverlag, 1978.

Hucker, Charles O., *China's Imperial Past.* Stanford, Calif.: Stanford University Press, 1975.

Ions, Veronica, *Indian Mythology* (Library of the World's Myths and Legends). New York: Peter Bedrick Books, 1984.

Irving, Clive, *Crossroads of Civilization: 3000 Years of Persian History.* New York: Barnes & Noble Books, 1979.

The Jerusalem Bible. Garden City, New York: Doubleday, 1966.

Johnson, David George, *The Medieval Chinese Oligarchy.* Boulder, Colo.: Westview Press, 1977.

Jones, A. H. M.:
The Decline of the Ancient World. New York: Holt, Rinehart and Winston, 1966.
The Later Roman Empire 284–602, Vol. 1. Baltimore: The Johns Hopkins University Press, 1986.

Kähler, Heinz, *Hagia Sophia.* Transl. by Ellyn Childs. New York: Frederick A. Praeger, 1967.

Kalidasa, *Shakuntala and Other Writings.* Transl. by Arthur W. Ryder. New York: E. P. Dutton, 1959.

Karnapp, Walter, *Die Stadtmauer Von Resafa in Syrien.* Vol. 11 in *Denkmäler Antiker Architektur.* Berlin, West Germany: Walter de Gruyter, 1976.

Katz, Friedrich, *The Ancient American Civilizations.* Transl. by K. M. Lois Simpson. New York: Praeger, 1972.

Kinross, Lord, and the Editors of the Newsweek Book Division, *Hagia Sophia.* New York: Newsweek, 1972.

Kitzinger, Ernst:
Byzantine Art in the Making. Cambridge, Mass.: Harvard University Press, 1977.
Early Medieval Art in the British Museum & British Library. London: British Museum Publications, 1983.

Kraeling, Carl H., *The Synagogue.* New Haven, Conn.: Yale University Press, 1956.

Kubler, George, *The Art and Architecture of Ancient America.* Harmondsworth, Middlesex, England: Penguin Books, 1984.

Laiou, Angeliki E., *Constantinople and the Latins.* Cambridge, Mass.: Harvard University Press, 1972.

Lancaster, Osbert, *Sailing to Byzantium.* Boston: Gambit Inc., 1969.

Leacroft, Helen, and Richard Leacroft, *The Buildings of Byzantium.* London: Hodder & Stoughton and Addison-Wesley Publishing Co., 1977.

Lee, Sherman E., *A History of Far Eastern Art.* Englewood Cliffs, N.J. / New York: Prentice-Hall and Harry N. Abrams, 1973.

Leonard, Jonathan Norton, and the Editors of Time-Life Books, *Ancient America* (Great Ages of Man series). New York: Time-Life Books, 1967.

Lissner, Ivar, *The Caesars: Might and Madness.* Transl. by J. Maxwell Brownjohn. New York: Capricorn Books, 1965.

L'Orange, Hans Peter, *The Roman Empire: Art Forms and Civic Life.* New York: Rizzoli, 1985.

Lumbreras, Luis G., *The Peoples and Cultures of Ancient Peru.* Transl. by Betty J. Meggers. Washington, D.C.: Smithsonian Institution Press, 1974.

McCabe, Joseph, *The Empresses of Constantinople.* London: Methuen & Co., 1913.

McNeill, William H.:
The Rise of the West. Chicago, Ill.: The University of Chicago Press, 1964.
A World History. New York: Oxford University Press, 1979.

Maenchen-Helfen, J. Otto, *The World of the Huns.* Berkeley, Calif.: University of California Press, 1973.

Maity, Sachindra Kumar, *The Imperial Guptas and Their Times.* New Delhi: Munshiram Manoharlal Publishers Pvt. Ltd., 1975.

Majumdar, R. C.:
Ancient India. Delhi: Motilal Banarsidass, 1982.
Hindu Colonies in the Far East. Calcutta: Firma K. L. Mukhopadhyay, 1963.

Mango, Cyril:
Byzantine Architecture. New York: Harry N. Abrams, 1976.
Le Développement Urbain de Constantinople. Paris: Diffusion De Boccard, 1985.
Materials for the Study of St. Sophia at Istanbul. Washington, D.C.: The Dumbarton Oaks Research Library and Collection / Trustees for Harvard University, 1962.

Martindale, J. R., *The Prosopography of the Later Roman Empire: A.D. 395-527.* Vol. 2. Cambridge: Cambridge University Press, 1980.

Mathews, Thomas F., *The Byzantine Churches of Istanbul.* University Park, Pa.: The Pennsylvania University Press, 1976.

Matthews, John, *Western Aristocracies and Imperial Court: A.D. 364-425.* London: Clarendon Press, 1975.

Meyer, Michael C., and William L. Sherman, *The Course of Mexican History.* New York: Oxford University Press, 1983.

Michell, George, *The Hindu Temple.* New York: Harper & Row, 1977.

Moore, Albert C., *Iconography of Religions.* London: SCM Press Ltd., 1977.

Musset, Lucien, *The Germanic Invasions.* Transl. by Edward James and Columba James. University Park, Pa.: The Pennsylvania State University Press, 1975.

Nicholson, H. B., ed., *Origins of Religious Art & Iconography in Preclassic Mesoamerica.* Los Angeles: UCLA Latin American Center Publications / Ethnic Arts Council of Los Angeles, 1976.

The Oxford Classical Dictionary. Edited by N. G. L. Hammond and H. H. Scullard. Oxford: Clarendon Press, 1970.

Pasztory, Esther, *The Murals of Tepantitla, Teotihuacan.* New York: Garland Publishing, 1976.

Pasztory, Esther, ed., *Middle Classic Mesoamerica: A.D. 400-700.* New York: Columbia University Press, 1978.

Perkins, Ann, *The Art of Dura-Europos.* Oxford: Oxford University Press, 1973.

Previté-Orton, C. W., *The Later Roman Empire to the Twelfth Century.* Vol. 1 of *The Shorter Cambridge Medieval History.* London: Cambridge University Press, 1952.

Randers-Pehrson, Justine Davis, *Barbarians and Romans.* Norman, Okla.: University of Oklahoma Press, 1983.

Reichel-Dolmatoff, G., *Columbia* (Ancient Peoples and Places series). New York: Frederick A. Praeger, 1965.

Resafa I, by Michael Mackensen (Deutsches Archäologisches Institut. Mainz am Rhein: Verlag Phillip Von Zabern, 1984.

Resafa II, by Thilo Ulbert (Deutsches Archäologisches Institut). Mainz am Rhein: Verlag Phillip Von Zabern, 1984.

Ronnen, Meir, *Jerusalem: Cité Biblique.* Paris: Editions Vilo, 1968.

Rostovtzeff, M., *Dura-Europos and Its Art.* Oxford: Oxford University Press, 1938.

Sackville-West, V., *Poems of West & East.* London: John Lane Co., 1918.

Sanpaolesi, Piero, *La Chiesa di S. Sophia a Constantinopli.* Rome: Officina Edizioni, 1978.

Schele, Linda, and Mary Ellen Miller, *The Blood of Kings: Dynasty and Ritual in Maya Art.* New York / Fort Worth: George Braziller / Kimbell Art Museum, 1986.

Schulberg, Lucille, and the Editors of Time-Life Books, *Historic India* (Great Ages of Man series). Alexandria, Va.: Time-Life Books, 1979.

Shahid, Irfan, *Byzantium and the Arabs in the Fourth Century.* Washington, D.C.: Dumbarton Oaks / Trustees for Harvard University, 1984.

Shanks, Hershel, *Judaism in Stone.* New York / Washington, D.C.: Harper & Row / Biblical Archaeology Society, 1979.

Sherrard, Philip, *Constantinople: Iconography of a Sacred City.* London: Oxford University Press, 1965.

Sherrard, Philip, and the Editors of Time-Life Books, *Byzantium* (Great Ages of Man series). Alexandria, Va.: Time-Life Books, 1980.

Simons, Gerald, and the Editors of Time-Life Books, *Barbarian Europe* (Great Ages of Man series). New York: Time-Life Books, 1968.

Simson, Otto G. von, *Sacred Fortress: Byzantine Art and Statecraft in Ravenna.* Chicago, Ill.: The University of Chicago Press, 1948.

Singh, Madanjeet, *Ajanta.* Lausanne, Switzerland: Edita, 1965.

Smith, Bradley, *Mexico: A History in Art.* Garden City, N.Y.: Doubleday, 1968.

Spink, Walter, *Ajanta to Ellora.* Bombay: Marg Publications The Center for South and Southeast Asian Studies, no date.

Stevenson, J., *The Catacombs.* London: Thames and Hudson, 1978.

Strong, Donald, *Roman Art.* Harmondsworth, Middlesex, England: Penguin Books, 1980.

Tarzi, Zemaryalai, *L'Architecture et le Décor Rupestre des Grottes de Bamiyan.* Paris: Imprimerie Nationale, 1977.

Thakur, Upendra, *The Hūnas in India.* Vol. 18 of *The Chowkhamba Sanskrit Studies.* Varanasi, India: The Chowkhamba Sanskrit Series Office, 1967.

Thomas, Hugh, *A History of the World.* New York: Harper Colophon Books, 1982.

Thompson, E. A.:
The Early Germans. Oxford: Clarendon Press, 1965.
A History of Attila and the Huns. Oxford: Clarendon Press, 1948.
Romans and Barbarians. Madison, Wis.: The University of Wisconsin Press, 1982.
The Visigoths in the Time of Ulfila. Oxford: Clarendon Press, 1966.

Thompson, J. Eric S., *The Rise and Fall of Maya Civilization.* Norman, Okla.: University of Oklahoma Press, 1955.

Wallace-Hadrill, *The Barbarian West.* New York: Harper Torchbooks, 1962.

Walsh, Michael, *Roots of Christianity.* London: Grafton Books, 1986.

Watson, Francis, *A Concise History of India.* London: Thames and Hudson, 1981.

Watson, William, *Art of Dynastic China.* London: Thames and Hudson, 1981.

Weaver, Muriel Porter, *The Aztecs, Maya, and Their Predecessors.* New York: Academic Press, 1981.

Weiner, Sheila L., *Ajanta: Its Place in Buddhist Art.* Berkeley, Calif.: University of California Press, 1977.

Welch, Holmes, *Taoism: The Parting of the Way.* Boston: Beacon Press, 1965.

Wenzel, Marian, *Finding Out about the Byzantines* (Exploring the Past series). London: Frederick Muller Ltd., 1965.

Wightman, Edith Mary:
Gallia Belgica. Berkeley, Calif.: University of California Press, 1985.
Roman Trier and the Treveri. New York: Praeger, 1971.

Wolpert, Stanley, *A New History of In-*

dia. New York: Oxford University Press, 1982.

Wright, Arthur F.:
Buddhism in Chinese History. New York: Atheneum, 1967.
The Sui Dynasty. New York: Alfred A. Knopf, 1978.

Wu-chi Liu and Irving Yucheng Lo, eds., *Sunflower Splendor.* Garden City, N.Y.: Anchor Books, 1975.

Yang Hsüan-chih, *A Record of Buddhist Monasteries in Lo-yang.* Transl. by Yi-t'ung Wang. Princeton, N.J.: Princeton University Press, 1984.

Yarshater, Ehsan, ed., *The Seleucid, Parthian and Sasanian Periods.* Vol. 3 (2) of *The Cambridge History of Iran.* Cambridge: Cambridge University Press, 1983.

Zimmer, Heinrich, *The Art of Indian Asia* (Bollingen series 33). Vol. 1. Princeton, N.Y.: Princeton University

Press, 1983.

Zürcher, E., *The Buddhist Conquest of China.* Leiden, Holland: E. J. Brill,|1972.

PERIODICALS

Angier, Natalie, "New Clues to the Maya Mystery." *Discover,* June 1981.

Aveni, Anthony F., "The Nazca Lines: Patterns in the Desert." *Archaeology,* July / August 1986.

Hammond, Norman, "The Discovery of Tikal." *Archaeology,* May / June 1987.

Justeson, John S., "The Origin of Writing Systems: Preclassic Mesoamerica." *World Archaeology,* Feb. 1986.

McIntyre, Loren, "Mystery of the Ancient Nazca Lines." *National Geographic,* May 1985.

Morell, Virginia, "The Lost Language of Cobá." *Science 86,* Mar. 1986.

Vann, Lindley, "The Palace and Gardens of Kasayapa at Sigiriya, Sri Lanka." *Archaeology,* July / August 1987.

OTHER SOURCES

Chandra, Pramod, *The Sculpture of India: 3000 B.C.–1300 A.D.* Washington, D.C.: National Gallery of Art, 1985.

Chine: Trésors et Splendeurs. Montreal: Les Editions Arthaud, 1986.

The Quest for Eternity: Chinese Ceramic Sculptures from the People's Republic of China. Los Angeles / San Francisco: Los Angeles County Museum of Art / Chronicle Books, 1987.

Thorp, Robert L., and Virginia Bower, *Spirit and Ritual: The Morse Collection of Ancient Chinese Art.* New York: The Metropolitan Museum of Art, 1982.

Weitzman, Kurt, ed., *Age of Spirituality.* New York: The Metropolitan Museum of Art / Princeton University Press, 1979.

PICTURE CREDITS